THE ROAD TO
NOWHERE

THE ROAD TO
NOWHERE

MEMORIES

Newfoundland and Labrador

Cyril Goodyear

St. John's, Newfoundland and Labrador
2004

Le Conseil des Arts | The Canada Council
du Canada | for the Arts

We acknowledge the support of The Canada Council for the Arts for our
publishing program.

We acknowledge the financial support of the Government of Canada through the
Book Publishing Industry Development Program (BPIDP) for our
publishing program.

∞ Printed on acid-free paper

Published by
CREATIVE PUBLISHERS
an imprint of CREATIVE BOOK PUBLISHING
a division of Creative Printers and Publishers Limited
a Print Atlantic associated company
P.O. Box 8660, St. John's, Newfoundland and Labrador A1B 3T7

First Edition
Typeset in 12 point New Baskerville

Printed in Canada by:
PRINT ATLANTIC

National Library of Canada Cataloguing in Publication

Goodyear, Cyril, 1926-
    The road to nowhere / Cyril Goodyear.

ISBN 1-894294-69-6

    1. Goodyear, Cyril, 1926- 2. Newfoundland and Labrador--Biography.
I. Title.

FC2174.1.G66A3 2004   971.8'04'092   C2004-900034-9

DEDICATION

This book is dedicated to all the former members of the Newfoundland Ranger Force and their spouses who made such an outstanding contribution to their people and country during the period July 1935 to July 31, 1950. That organization was disbanded by Order of the Government of the Province of Newfoundland, presided over by Premier J.R. Smallwood, subsequent to Newfoundland becoming part of Canada on April 1, 1949. While the 'history' of the organization is said to have been written in subsequent years, full credit for their feats and loyalty has never been given to the men of the Force, or the women who supported them and our people in so many ways.

True, there is an official history authored by Harold Horwood; but it is not generally known that the Newfoundland Ranger Force Association provided him with the basic research, and paid him to write it. I was a member of the committee which dealt with these matters. One would have thought that he would have filled in the gaps by interviewing as many former members as possible, and scrutinized the reasoning behind the decision to disband the Force. He did neither, and as a result those who remain struggle to present the facts. It is unfortunate that those who write accurate accounts, based on their personal experience and knowledge, seem to have less credibility than those who have no personal experience and offer fiction and inaccuracy as fact. The novel, *The White Eskimo*, is a prime example.

Fifteen years is a short life for any person or organization, but within that time frame members of the Force did an incredible job. In 1935 the minimum educational standard for recruits was Grade Eleven. There were few per capita in Newfoundland, or even Canada, with those qualifications at that time. While the Force was 'modeled' on the Royal Canadian Mounted Police, it had higher entrance standards and was quite different in that it performed a multitude of duties in addition to police work. Following the suspension of the Constitution in 1933, and the creation of a Commission to govern Newfoundland and Labrador, members of the Force in the field provided the new government with regular accurate reports on all phases of social and economic activity in the country. These reports were the basis of government policy in the fifteen years of its existence. Perusal of Ranger Force documents in the Newfoundland and Labrador Archives will show the initials of all the Commissioners; a clear indication of their value. That was a period when there were no elected members from the districts, no town or village councils; only the Rangers between the people and the Commissioners in remote St. John's.

The period between April 1, 1949 and August 1, 1950 is a scant fifteen months. That is hardly sufficient for a new government to create a new bureaucracy with a multitude of new departments, and to make a major decision on changing the total policing system. The country had been divided between the Newfoundland Constabulary and the Newfoundland Rangers, with the latter policing and administering programs in the bulk of the country. In the year following Confederation, rumours began to circulate that the future of the Newfoundland Ranger Force was uncertain. Yet John Parsons, in his book *Probably Without Equal* says that the Rangers actively supported and promoted confederation with Canada.* That is news to me; perhaps there were some who became partisan, but my recollection is that our members were professionals who did their job and remained neutral. How we voted in the referenda was our business! If what he alleges was believed to be true, we were rewarded by being disbanded. That is hardly gratitude!

Newfoundland Ranger Detachment in Battle Harbour, Labrador.

As a matter of fact, without adequate notice or explanation, we were summoned to St. John's to be examined and assessed to see if we were suitable for engagement in the RCMP. In a bulletin, dated July 4, 1950, Chief Ranger E.L. Martin advised all members that he had been written by the then Attorney General, Leslie R. Curtis, that Commissioner Wood of the RCMP offered us positions in that Force, effective August 1, 1950, at reduced rank. We were instructed to reply immediately whether we would accept. He said that should we refuse to join the RCMP, government would not assist us in obtaining other employment. It should be noted that summer mail was delivered around Newfoundland and Labrador by train or ship. The time frame was very short for some of us.

I was married with a pregnant spouse and, like most others, had little choice. All but a few of us engaged in the RCMP for the contract period of five years. As we integrated, it was somewhat of a relief to us that all we had to do was police work. I don't recall that we were ever thanked for our prior service to our country, except during a speech by Premier Smallwood, subsequent to our demise.

When the evidence is assessed, it will be obvious that the decision to disband our organization was made during the negotiations on the Terms of Union with Canada. There is no way it could have been planned and put in place in that short fifteen month time frame. Nor could that decision have been based on economics. After the Ranger Force was disbanded, it was replaced by many members of the RCMP, and us, plus a small army of Federal and Provincial civil servants. Because of the unpopularity of Confederation, a decision was made to replace us with what was touted as an 'apolitical' symbol, the Royal Canadian Mounted Police, while at the same time blanketing the new Province with people loyal to Canada. That is a standard policy of occupying powers. We were cut down in the prime of our organizational life, and sacrificed on the altar of political expediency. The Newfoundland Constabulary was shrunk back to the city of St. John's, where they languished in utter neglect until we reorganized the policing system in the Province during the rein of Premier Brian Peckford. True, we were absorbed into that other organization, but they could not have survived without us in the first few years.

This little book is one of the ways in which we highlight the legacy of the Newfoundland Ranger Force and its people. They have pursued fabulous careers in every organization and occupation in which they served, and since in retirement. They are an example to many others, juniors and seniors alike, who have little faith in their worth. This is especially so for those seniors who have come to believe that they have nothing to contribute, allowing all their hard earned knowledge and skills to shrink in the space of their minds, and to be lost to their communities and country.

The thing that bothers me most is that after we and those who know us well are gone, succeeding generations may come to believe that the Newfoundland Ranger Force was disbanded because it was inferior to the Royal Canadian Mounted Police. The facts clearly establish that nothing could be further from the truth!

* See *Probably Without Equal* by John Parsons, Grassy Pond Publishing, Shearstown, NL.

ACKNOWLEDGMENTS

I am most grateful to the current publisher, Dwayne LaFitte, the former publisher, Dawn Roche and the staff of Creative Book Publishing for their support, encouragement and advice during the difficult time I experienced since beginning this book. No one could have treated me better. I also want to thank the many other people who encouraged me, as well as the characters in the book, good and bad, who made it possible. As indicated, the actual cases can be researched by those who may have an interest. The characters are all real, except perhaps those in outer space; who can be sure? It is all part of a mind broadening exercise, like *Star Trek*. Without speculation and fantasy we would not progress.

As is the case with my other books, *Nunatsuak* and *Against the Elements*, I donate all royalties to The Eric Normore Memorial Foundation. That Foundation perpetuates the memory of a local war hero who gave his life, like many others, that we might enjoy the peace and freedom that we now experience. It is an incorporated charitable foundation, registered with the Canadian Customs & Revenue Service, and donations are tax deductible. I again invite you to make a donation to this worthy cause. The address is: The Eric Normore Memorial Foundation, 9 Church Street, Deer Lake, NL, A8A 1C9.

I thank you all most sincerely for your support and hope you enjoy interesting, long and productive lives. May your curiosity about life never falter.

Cyril J. Goodyear
Deer Lake, NL.
September 25, 2003

CONTENTS

INTRODUCTION

The theme of this little book is SPACE; space in its broadest sense. To think, write or speak about space in any other way would negate the concept. No one can afford to take a narrow view of space, especially those who seek to determine the true origin of the various species. Sometimes those believed to have the greatest minds ignore the lessons of space, including what has happened in our own time, and base their thinking on the premise that all life started on this planet.

We can shrink space in many ways. For example, when I first went to school the room seemed huge to me; filled with little people whom I didn't really know, and who seemed to invade my space at every turn. But I also had a lot of empty space in my head, which the teacher was determined to fill.

When the teacher, Melba Morey, assigned my desk, it was right up front in open space where every other kid could watch me. Now I couldn't scratch myself, put my finger in my nose or hide the fact that I was left-handed. I couldn't turn my head to see my fellow pupils; just strain my eyes right and left. It was agony for a poorly dressed kid of the 'Great Depression' knowing that the total class could watch every move I made.

But after a week of discomfort it was almost as if someone had put one-way glass walls around my desk. I began to feel like I was in my own little room; mind you I could look out and hear everything that was going on, but I lost the feeling that I was exposed to every eye in the place. I began to act normally; even picked my nose in an unconscious way occasionally. Now, all these years later, I feel the same way on my own property when I sit on the lawn in full sight of the neighbors and all those people who pass by on the street. You see we humans, and all other animals of whatever kind, have a built-in psychological mechanism for shrinking and expanding space no matter where we are. It's an internal gadget which makes us feel safe and comfortable; surrounded by the familiar. We even have the ability to sit or stand, exposed to the most magnificent view and 'be lost in the space of our minds'; not really seeing anything.

Except for our minds, or at least some minds, space always has limits. Canoeing across a lake provides the spatial boundary of the other shore. When I used to travel by dog team in northern Labrador, the ice seemed to stretch out, and the point receded. The slow pace of travel, and the extreme cold, made the distance to that point of land seem endless.

When we look out to sea from the beach, the horizon is the limit of space. But if we look at the same stretch of ocean from the top of a mountain, the horizon is farther away in space.

The Vikings, Columbus, Cabot, Cook and many thousands of their predecessors and successors have covered the vast surface spaces of the oceans. Others have plumbed the less known spaces under the seas and oceans in an ever increasing array of submarines. Lesser mortals enlarge their understanding of under-ocean space by the now simple method of scuba diving.

From a jet plane space becomes more extended as we look up, down and all around. The Wright brothers,

Lindbergh and numerous others have allowed us to enter the vast space of the earth's atmosphere. We travel daily on aircraft throughout the earth and take it for granted; another dimension in the continuing conquest of space.

When we think of cosmonauts Yuri Gagarin and Gherman Titov, as well as astronauts John Glenn, Neil Armstrong and Buzz Aldrin, and all their successors, we believe that these men and women really understand space. It is certainly true that those who have left the earth and travelled millions of kilometres/miles in space have a greater understanding of it; both in their minds and souls. Armstrong and Aldrin, the first two earthlings who walked on the moon, that we know of, can probably never adequately explain their experience. For, to quote Kahil Gibran, "Thought is truly a bird of space, but when surrounded by a cage of words, can indeed spread its wings; but cannot fly."

In our time the ultimate form and freedom of space exploration is the space shuttle. It blasts off almost routinely and docks with the space station. The astronauts 'walk' and work in space. But really in concept it is not much different than when I was in school, or travelling in a car, boat, submarine or airplane.

In September 2002, I travelled on Mel Woodward's oil tanker *Mokami* from Long Pond to Iqaluit on Baffin Island; a distance of almost thirteen hundred straight line miles. It was a fantastic trip, in every respect. The weather was marginal and we travelled for days in an inverted bowl of fog. We could look out to the rim of the 'bowl', but not beyond, for the 'bowl' moved with us. There was nothing in sight but sea and the occasional seabird and fog. For twenty-four hours a day the only sounds were the pulsing throb of the engine and other internal noises. Outside was the pounding sea, running and splashing and spraying everything from scupper to antenna. Inside, those on watch worked away. The rest of us ate, read, talked, slept and took our daily walks around deck in suitable clothes. We were the only people in the world, seemingly; except those ghostly voices on marine radio. We were out in space; the only difference was the 'vehicle' and the 'medium'. All living things must have 'life support systems' whether they are stationary, or in motion; travelling through the 'time-space' of their lives.

Once humans overcame the cultural restrictions of their minds, and the fear of being off the ground, it was inevitable that the genetic seeds of knowledge would be allowed to grow, expand and adapt the earthbound concepts of space to 'outer space'.

All space travellers are confined to their small vehicles, or tied to them when they go outside; and in addition they orbit, i.e. 'go around in circles.' It is a larger hoop; a merry-go-round.

Some day, as we continue to develop the technology which is in genetic memory, and with the demonstrated experience of the past, we will undoubtedly travel vast distances in space; stopping occasionally to orbit and visit nearby planets, and then move on. Perhaps we will meet our clansmen and cousins in the far reaches of space on other planets. But in the meantime the greatest expanse of space is in our minds; perhaps the only truly 'limitless space.'

At my age, I have neither much time nor space left. Thus I invite the reader to explore the many dimensions of space between the covers of THE ROAD TO NOWHERE. While the stories are varied, sometimes seemingly disconnected, they all have a connection to the theme; however tenuously.

It is your challenge, as a reader and thinker, to discover that connection.

Photo by Shirley Goodyear

Author Cyril Goodyear.

By the way, it is a fact that I met Yuri Gagarin, the first earthling in space, just the way Uncle Cy tells the story to Sarah.

Think About Your World

Did I ever tell you, how simple life can be,
When you look on everything; human, bird, or tree,
As something that lives, or has lived,
On Earth in some other form;
Or perhaps came from outer space,
Their wonders to perform.
And if we let our thoughts roam free,
It all becomes the norm.

If we are too self-centered,
Or our beliefs are frozen,
We become the mental prisoners,
Of the thoughts that we have chosen.
But if our minds are open,
To let new thoughts pass through,
We will begin every day,
Like a tourist seeing new.

What if the different races,
Living on this earth,
Were immigrants from outer space,
Who left their place of birth,
On some other planets,
Similar to ours,
Because of wars, or other cause,
Beyond their human powers?

Perhaps the black, the white, the brown,
The red, and shades of yellow,
Had no other place to go,
Where living was so mellow.
And in the distant memories,
In our seed and brains,
Some day we will remember,
Who came, and who remains.

We all look to the heavens,
Our thoughts are in the skies,
And somewhere in our memories,
Awaits a big surprise.
Because the great Creator,
Established more than Earth,
And we, the many races,
Must learn how much we're worth.

For we may be a tiny 'tad'
Of what is our estimation,
In terms of human, or other, life,
The sum of all Creation.
So let us open up our minds,
Especially when we're young,
And talk about the universe,
In every land and tongue.

The Car-i-boo Song

Sandy Lake is one of five large lakes that make up most of the watershed of the Humber Valley. The others are Birchy, Sheffield, Grand and Hinds. They flow out of the Long Range Mountains on the west coast of Newfoundland and into each other. How big do you think they are? Well, from the upper end of Birchy to the lower end of Grand Lake it is 120 miles, or almost 194 kilometres; a long way Hosea!

Up from the shores of Sandy Lake, as far as your eye can see, there stretches a high barren part of the mountains known as the Topsails. When you look at the high peaks from a certain position, they seem like giant sails on a huge schooner; that's how the mountains got their name. Herds of caribou have roamed around and across the Topsails from the beginning of time. They feed on the moss and other lichens, sleep by the small lakes and play hide-and-seek amongst the big boulders left there by the glaciers when they passed through.

It is a wonderful place with lots of berries in the summer to feed the wild geese, bears and small birds. Foxes and ptarmigan frighten each other when they get the chance. Trout jump and play between the raindrops on summer evenings in the small lakes. Field mice run quickly from bush to rock, not saying a word to anyone because they are so timid. I always speak to them, even if I don't see them; it makes them feel better you know. You see animals are like people; they like to be spoken to in a friendly way. However, don't let your friends hear you speaking to a mouse you can't see; they may think you a bit odd.

My name is Tom; it's not official, but my Mother always called me Tom and I guess it stuck to me. In some quarters I am also known as Uncle Cy. Not because I sigh a lot but because I'm usually too busy to be melancholy.

I often paddle my canoe around the shore of Sandy Lake, and up Kitty's Brook. Sometimes when I am camped there amongst the driftwood, a big stag caribou will walk along shore, just to see what I'm doing. He'll look for a while, and then wander off thinking I am crazy to live in a tent when I could be outdoors all the time. We never discuss our lifestyles; it would not be polite. Sometimes in winter I drive my snowmobile over the frozen lake and up the fringe of woods between the lake and the Topsails to see what the caribou are doing. I'm just as curious as they are!

Not long ago, I drove alongshore and up near Kitty's Brook. As I approached the big bog which runs out by the brook, I spotted thirteen caribou; an unlucky number, you think. They were walking along over the drifted snow taking their time and, I suppose, talking to each other. The wind was blowing from the west towards me. I parked the snowmobile under a big drift out of sight. It looked to me like they were going to walk up through an open lead in the woods from the bog and on up to the Topsails. Taking my time, I walked to the edge of the spruce trees where I could watch them. They were about a kilometre away when all of a sudden they turned around and faced into the wind. It didn't seem to make sense, but then I saw three more caribou coming towards them.

A young caribou.

They obviously smelled the three other caribou who were coming up-wind. Like us, caribou have their own general odour, and each one has some little smell which makes it different from the others. Out there, in the clear fresh air, odorous are more easily detectable. You can smell cigarette smoke a long way off. In the cities there are so many smells you can break wind while standing in a crowd and they won't know it. If you don't believe me try it sometime. When the three caribou caught up with them, they all turned around and came towards me.

When they came within 100 metres or so, I stepped out of the trees with my hands up to the sides of my head, like antlers. They stopped and looked, and looked. Now caribou have poor eyesight; there are no eye doctors in their society to look after them. Maybe they thought at first I was a stray caribou. Anyway, they didn't say anything but must have decided I was different and started to walk away.

Author's photo

A friendly caribou.

I wanted to look at them a little longer; what was I to do? There was no one else within miles, so I started to sing. It came right out of me, a caribou inspired song!

There was a young CAR-I-BOO ,
Out on the BOG.
He fell on his BUM,
When he slipped on a LOG.
But he didn't stay down there very long,
And that is the end of my CAR-I-BOO song.

Over and over again I sang and shouted 'The Car-I-Boo Song.' They looked and looked and shuffled their feet as if a little bit embarrassed at not being able to applaud. I must confess I got carried away with the sheer excitement of it.

If you had been nearby and saw this strange man sprouting 'hand-like' antlers and singing at the top of his lungs from a large snowdrift, you would have said he was crazy. But the caribou didn't think I was crazy. They appreciated a little entertainment and nodded and bowed their heads, laughing silently while the vapour from their nostrils wafted away in the cold wind.

Perhaps later, they thought about it and discussed it, because every group of living beings has their own language. That we don't hear or understand it, does not alter that fact. Maybe they thought I was crazy, but decided it was not their problem. Had it been one of them acting irrationally, they might have banished him; just like we used to do not many years ago.

It is too bad I couldn't think of another suitable song to sing to them, because, like all people being entertained, they wanted variety. One song, repeated over and over again became a little boring. They lowered their heads and shuffled their feet and started to move away. Louder singing did not attract them.

Realizing that my performance was over, because it all depends on the interest of the audience, I shouted, "I'll see you on the Topsails. I'll see you on the Topsails!" The sixteen caribou paused and looked around, trying to grasp what I was saying. I said again, "Look for me up on the Topsails!"

As if understanding, or perhaps being polite, the caribou nodded their heads, clicked their antlers, blew vapour from their noses and turned away to make the long climb. Up there they looked out over the vast spaces of the snow covered barrens and saw the jets passing on their way to Deer Lake Airport. They didn't think any more about airplanes than the stars, moon and northern lights. After all these were common things in their lifetime.

Uncle Jim and the Crow

Uncle Jim loved crows. Ever since he was a little boy growing up on the farm. There were dozens of them nesting in the nearby trees, and they made regular visits to the barn. Uncle Jim used to throw stones at them at first, but his mother told him he had no need to fear crows as they were part of the work force on the farm. After that he used to watch them with interest as they made their regular rounds. They would "caw" to him and he would "caw" back. After a while it was as if they understood each other.

He would watch them fly around by themselves, or in pairs. Sometimes they would meet in a large group on the edge of the cornfield, strutting and talking; almost like they were having a conference or a church service.

When the little crows were born he would climb the ladder to the barn roof and watch the parents feed them. Later they taught them how to fly. Jim said to his mother one day, "Mom, those crows look after their babies almost like you do. They're a lot like us." Jim's Mom nodded wisely, but didn't say much else. She was glad that Jim was learning something new about the world every day.

As Jim grew up he got more interested in the crows and could tell his schoolmates all about them. Jim talked to the crows all the time. Now you may wonder how the word 'caw' can mean so many things. I really can't explain it but Jim and the crows clearly understood each other. They used to land alongside him, no matter what he was doing, and "caw" continuously. Sometimes one of the neighbors or their visitors would shoot a crow. Jim always told the other crows and they would gather round while he buried it respectfully in the corner of the barnyard. His mother often told him that all animals and birds had a place in society and everybody should respect them. Jim knew this was right, for after all, didn't his favorite crow wake him up every morning at the same time by flapping his wings on the roof over Jim's bedroom. He used to "caw" gently three or four times.

Jim left the farm and went on to university. Afterwards, he worked as an engineer and lived in the city. However, his work often took him out in the country and he talked to the crows every chance he got. Even the strange crows seemed to trust him after a while. After all, just think about it, dogs and horses understand English or French or whatever language their owners speak. The problem is that owners don't try to speak dog, horse or other animal languages. It is not that animals are smarter than humans; they just don't take anything for granted, but try all the time.

Later, when Jim got married, he tried to get his wife interested in crows but she didn't have the same background. Growing up in the city sometimes means you don't meet many crows. Jim and his wife had a little girl, Sarah, and Jim was determined she should learn as much about wildlife as possible, especially crows. All the while she was growing up he would take her to parks and farms. On camping trips she learned to love the birds and animals, almost as much as he did. Also, she was fascinated by the stars and heard all the myths about the planets.

He never got tired of explaining to Sarah that birds and animals were not much different from people; they only looked and talked different. In fact, when she was old enough, he explained that people of the Buddhist religion believed that after people died their spirits came back to earth in some other form. It was, he explained, another form of immortality; that is, living forever. Every religion teaches the same thing in some way or other. Jim always told Sarah that, if the Buddhists were right, he would like to come back as a crow. He and Sarah used to laugh a lot about that, but her mother was not amused.

Jim lived to a ripe old age, having bought a house in the country after he retired. He renewed his friendship with the crows and spent many a happy time talking with them in his back garden. Sarah and her husband visited regularly, as she was very close to her father. They spent many a pleasant weekend watching all the aerobatics in the back garden. It was better than having the 'Snowbirds' put on a personal show.

Uncle Jim passed away, as all old people must; no matter how sad it may seem. Sarah had many memories to console her. Memories were made for that purpose; it was a way of recordings things before the camera and photographs and movies.

One day, about six months after her father passed away, Sarah was sitting by the patio door having a cup of tea and thinking about her father. A big crow flew up and landed on the patio rail. It looked at her for a time and then, with a flick of his wings, landed by the door. The crow looked at her intently, moving its head from side to side to get a good view, said "caw" and then flew away.

Every day after that, when she was home, the crow came and did the same thing. Sometimes it would peck at the door. After a while Sarah began to feed it. She always had a strange feeling that her father was near whenever the crow came. They talked to each other in the Crow language.

One spring day the crow came, and Sarah noticed that one of its left toes was bent over. 'Just like my father's,' she thought; and on his left foot too. You see, when Jim was a child he broke the little toe on his left foot. Because there was no doctor, his toe remained twisted after it healed.

Each day thereafter she looked for that twisted toe. There was no doubt that the same crow came every day. Sarah, though very doubtful, always had the feeling of nearness to her father when the crow came. After all, he always said, "I want to come back as a crow."

Now I knew Uncle Jim many years ago. While I can't say whether Uncle Jim got his wish or not, I do say this: "Always treat animals and birds as kindly as you can, because you never know who they might have been before."

The Scruffy Fir Tree

Did you ever think about what it would be like to be a tree, rather than a boy or girl? As children we learn to crawl, walk, talk, laugh, cry and associate with other people. We learn new things every day; what we can do in our lives is almost limitless. What about a tree? He or she will pop up through the ground, in the garden or forest, but no matter how big they grow they can never leave that spot unless someone uproots them or cuts them down.

The only other way they can move, in a small way, is when the wind blows or the snow falls on them. When people bump into them they move a little, but can't cry out in pain The only time they talk is when the wind causes them to rub together. I often hear trees talking when I am camped up country in my tent. It is comforting to hear their familiar voices.

Imagine that you are a tree! Along comes a moose and eats your tips; squirrels chew off your buds and let them fall to the ground. A caribou or moose scrapes his horns on you, or a passing fox or dog leaves a yellow stain. Birds build their nests on you, or stand on your head watching what is going on. You can't go indoors when it rains or snows. No matter how cold your feet get in winter, you can't go in to get warm. It is true that people can cut you down and burn you, or you can be destroyed in a forest fire; but that is not a good way to get warm. Perhaps, when you are cut down to make paper for books you might feel a little better about it. You see, it is not easy being a tree!

A junior and senior tree.

Just like people who are black, brown, red, yellow or white, trees look different too. Also, some kinds of trees like to live in different parts of the world; just like us. In Canada we are used to the bushy pine, the prickly spruce, the sticky fir and the soft friendly juniper. We love the birches and the shaky aspen. Even the obstinate alders interest us; even though when we walk through an alder grove they always come towards us, no matter how many times we change direction. How we stare in wonder at the maple trees, especially in the fall when they show off before the snow comes. Imagine losing your outer clothes when winter comes, like the maples and the birches.

Some trees are beautifully shaped, like Christmas trees. Others are twisted with broken limbs. Some are amongst their friends and relatives in the thick forest, so they never get lonely. It is sad when some of them have to look down all day at their parents, who lie on the ground as fallen logs and twisted stumps. Other trees stand alone on a point overlooking a lake or river, while some hang by their roots on the edge of a cliff. Whatever their position, they cannot move or change anything by themselves. How fortunate we are!

There is a lonely tree on a point overlooking the pond where I go to camp and fish. His limbs are twisted and you would not say, "That's a beautiful tree." But I see that tree in all kinds of weather, and he is almost like an old friend. Some days he drips rainwater and shivers in the cold wind. I often sit in my tent and wish he could come in. Now I could bring him in; but I would have to kill him first, and that wouldn't do. So I say to him every now and then, when there is nobody around, "Don't worry, Old Buddy, summer will come soon and you will be warm again."

Last winter there was lots of snow, and strong winds. The first snow came and stuck to him, almost like a suit of white underwear. Over the next few weeks more snow fell and provided more layers; just like adding shirts and pants and sweaters, and he grew bigger and more healthy looking as the wind shaped him. Just think of someone you know who doesn't look all that handsome or pretty; but when they dress up, what a difference! Just like my friend, the Scruffy Fir Tree.

Anyway, when I went back in February to set up my winter tent, for the moment, I thought my friend was gone. But 'No', he was there alright, standing in the same place but dressed all in white; just like a snowman. I couldn't resist it, because we always try to improve everything. I put my woolen cap on his head, made a mouth, nose and

Author's photo

Tree dressed as a snowman

eyes of twigs and there he stood; a perfect living snowman.

The Friendly Ones

Little Tom was a friendly boy, or so everyone said. He would always smile and wave at people passing by. It didn't matter whether they were children or grownups. In fact he thought he liked grownups better because they would stop and talk to him, and sometimes give him a candy bar. His friends next door could hardly wait to come over and play because he was so pleasant.

Tom's Mom and Dad were just as friendly. In fact, when his Dad was mowing the lawn he would sometimes talk to passers-by so long that the lawn didn't get finished that day. His Mom was more business-like, but would still chat with everyone in the stores. She nearly always sensed when someone was lonely, or needed help, and would talk to complete strangers at any time. What most people don't think about, especially city folk, is that people are basically friendly; they just don't know how to approach others. Saying "Good Day" is the easiest way to do it. Even a remark that doesn't quite fit will do the trick.

Mosie Murrin, who was a 'street person' before people knew what a street person was, had a way of getting people's attention. One time he was on the dock in Corner Brook when a cruise ship came into port. As the tourists came down the gangway one of them said to Mosie, "Hello, are you from here?"

"Of course, " Mosie replied.

"Have you lived all your life in Newfoundland?" the tourist asked.

"Not yet," said Mosie.

The tourist was so taken by this unusual, but accurate reply, that he talked to Mosie for a long time. He then treated Mosie to a nice lunch in the Chinese Café; which was what Mosie wanted in the first place. You see, there are many ways to get people's attention.

There were two people who walked past Tom's house every morning. He always spoke to them but they never looked his way or made any reply. They nearly always dressed alike; or as much as they could for a man and a woman. In summer they would wear the same colour shorts and shirts. When it rained they wore identical raincoats. In the winter their pants, boots and coats matched. He could spot them plainly with their yellow parkas standing out against the pure white snow.

Try as often as he would, he could not get their attention. This bothered the friendly little boy, and he often spoke to his mother about it. She didn't know who they were, but had noticed that they always marched by without as much as a glance or a nod. "Don't worry about it, Tom," she said, "Some people are like that, whatever the reason. I don't know who they are, but I say to myself, there go the friendly ones."

One day in the spring, when the street was slippery, Tom was out on the driveway. Since they always came by at the same time every day, he waited patiently pretending to be breaking the ice near the road. When they passed by he spoke; but they marched on like two soldiers. Tom ran out on the street, skidded, and fell down in front of them. They were so surprised the man said, "Oh, my! Are your hurt?" Tom said timidly, "No, I just hoped you would speak to me." The were so surprised they just stood there for a while. Finally, the woman said, "My, I never thought about it. We don't have any children of our own." "You can talk to me every day," said Tom. The three of them chatted awkwardly for a few minutes.

After that they stopped and talked to Tom every time they passed. Occasionally, when they saw his Mom and Dad, they would say, "Hello." In time, because of Tom, they really became 'The Friendly Ones.'

Photo by Brian Goodyear

Cyril and Shirley Goodyear.

Blowing Out the Candle

We should never laugh at people because they don't look or talk like us. But we can always laugh; as long as we know about what, and why we are laughing. None of us are perfect, whether we are little girls and boys or grown-ups. Everybody has some defect; none of them are enough to allow us to look down on people. Laughter is a wonderful thing; I wouldn't attempt to explain its psychology.

Many years ago I was having lunch at a local boarding house. I used to go there all the time when I was travelling around my police district. There were four other people there: one was a travelling salesman, another was a school inspector, a Salvation Army officer and a taxi driver.

I was growing bald, and noticing my hair was getting very thin, the salesman made some 'smart' remark about it. Now, years later, I am completely bald and it doesn't bother me a bit. It is a fact of life as there are millions like me around the world. In fact, one of the most famous bald persons that I can think of is E.T. Did you ever wonder why the upper part of his head is so big?

I was very embarrassed then, and showed it, but as I looked around the table I noticed that every one of them had a defect. Apparently they were unaware of it, so I said, "There is no doubt about it, I will soon be completely bald. But have you thought about the fact that everybody has something wrong with them? You, Mr. Salesman, have two fingers missing from your left hand." He looked down in surprise, so I said, "It's not your fault. I'm sure it was a terrible accident." By now I had their attention, so I said, "Mr. School Inspector, you have bad eyes and wear glasses." He looked shocked so I said, "Captain, you have false teeth, but I have all my own teeth." The taxi driver was squirming, so I said, "You have big ears, and one of them is deaf." Knowing that they were all embarrassed I said, "I only point these things out to show you that I have fewer defects than you. Being bald does not handicap me in any way. Now let's admit to being imperfect and finish our lunch." All of these people became friends of mine later.

So you see, when you understand what is wrong with yourself and others, you can still have a bit of fun and laugh without feeling guilty. We are all normal, no matter what seems to be wrong with us. People have been fat, thin, cripple, twisted, unable to speak plainly, blind, deaf, and a host of other things since time began. I repeat, "No one is perfect!"

My friend, Bob Roy, told me a story many years ago. While I have not changed the actual tale, I have changed the setting and the names to appeal to local interest. The intent, as was the case when it was first told, is to have a bit of fun and send a message.

John and Mary were two young people who both worked at a time when people were not paid very well. It was in the days before dial telephones, television and the many things we take for granted. Like most young people in love, they were anxious to get married. However, they wanted to have their own home and there was no bank to lend them money; even if they had good salaries. So, what did they do? They saved their money and started to build a house. First they put down posts; no basement, and made the floor. About six months later they got the walls put up. A year later they were still trying to save money to put on the roof.

After about five years the house was mostly finished. It had a stove for heat, had some of the wiring done, but no electricity. The telephone was like you see in museums; a boxlike thing with a crank handle and a thing you put up to your ear. Their door bell was run by batteries.

They couldn't wait any longer and decided to get married. After the wedding and the reception in the church basement, they walked to their new home and went in. It was in the fall and quite dark. Because there was no electricity, John lit a candle. They sat down for a while and talked, then went into their bedroom to get ready for bed. Mary was quite shy, as new brides always are, so she popped into bed as quick as she could.

John was a little slower, but put on his pyjamas and hopped into bed. "John," Mary said, "Are you going to blow out the candle?" "Why don't you?" he said. Mary giggled and said, "No, it's a bit cold. You blow out the candle." John got out of bed and picked up the candle from the box they were using until they could afford furniture.

By a strange coincidence John and Mary had twisted lips. His was twisted to the left, and hers to the right. He blew on the candle, but the wind went off to the left and the candle continued to give light. He tried several times, but couldn't blow out the candle. He said, "Mary, I tried to blow out the candle and I couldn't. If you don't try, we'll never get to sleep tonight."

Mary got out of bed and took the candle from John. She blew to the right several times, but the candle wouldn't go out. "I tried to blow out the candle, and couldn't." John said, "I tried to blow out the candle I couldn't either. What will we do? We won't get to sleep tonight?" Mary said, "We'll have to call Maw."

They both went out to the telephone, and John rang Fourteen Longs and Two Shorts several times. Finally Maw answered. Now her top lip was twisted downward. She said, "Hello-o, who is this?"

"Maw, this is John here. You know we don't have electricity, but only a candle. I tried to blow out the candle but I couldn't" Mary was tight to him and said, "Yes, Maw, I also tried to blow out the candle, but couldn't. What will we do? We'll never get to bed tonight."

"I'll be right up," Maw said.

Finally, the doorbell rang; run by batteries, and John and Mary went to the door. "What's the problem?" said Maw. "I tried to blow out the candle, but couldn't," said Mary. "Yes," said John, "So did I," and he blew at the candle but the wind went off to the left again.

"Give me that candle!" said Maw. She took the candle and blew, but the wind went right down by the candle and it wouldn't go out. She tried several times. "My," she said, "I tried to blow out the candle and couldn't." "Yes," said John and Mary, both at the same time, "I also tried to blow out the candle, but couldn't," "What will we do?" said Mary. "We'll just have to call Paw," said Maw.

Maw cranked out Fourteen Longs and Two Shorts on the old telephone. After several tries Paw answered, "Hello-o-o there. What do you want?" His bottom lip was twisted upward. "This is Maw, up at John and Mary's. Come up and blow out the candle or nobody will get to sleep tonight." "Up-p!" said Paw, "The night is almost over anyhow. I'll be up as soon as I can."

John, Mary and Maw waited a long time. John even had to put a couple of junks of wood in the stove. Finally, the doorbell rang, run by batteries, and Paw marched in. "Give me that candle!" he said. He took the candle and gave a big blow. But because of his mouth the wind blew upwards, and the candle continued to burn brightly. He tried it several times without success. They all walked around the candle on the box, in turn saying, "I tried to blow out the candle, but couldn't. What will we do? There'll be no sleep tonight."

Finally, Maw said, "We'll have to call Father Brown. He'll know what to do." It was agreed, and Maw called the Priest. She cranked out One Long and Fourteen Shorts. As her arm was getting tired, Father Brown answered the phone. "Hello," he said. "Is someone sick?" You see he was used to being called at all hours. "No, Father," Maw said. "We are up here at John and Mary's. You remember you married them today? "Oh, yes," he said, "What is the problem?" John spoke up. "Father, please come up. You know we don't have any electricity, just a candle. I tried to blow it out but couldn't." Mary, Maw and Paw all spoke up. "Yes, Father," they said. "We tried to blow out the candle too, but couldn't. Come up, we don't know what to do."

After quite a while the doorbell rang, run by batteries, and Father Brown came in. "Let me have the candle," he said. Mary passed the candle to him, and he looked at it for a while. They noticed that there was nothing wrong with his mouth. Finally, he put the tips of his thumb and finger in his mouth, and then pinched out the flame. John, Mary, Maw and Paw stood there in amazement. Finally, Paw said, "My Goodness, what it is to have education!"

The Star

Saturn is a huge planet in our solar system; ten times as big as this Earth. However, Saturn is three times farther from the Sun than Earth. Now you might think that the people on Saturn find it colder than we do because they are farther away from the Sun. I really don't know, but perhaps the huge size of Saturn allows it to catch and hold more heat.

Why do you think it is called Saturn? Really, it is because the people there 'sit' all the time. The first people sat, and rarely got up after that; so they called their home 'Sat-urn'. Of course they had to get up and move around sometimes or they wouldn't be able to get anything to eat; or even go to the bathroom. But they preferred to sit and invented and built nice chairs to make sitting more comfortable.

Many thousands, perhaps millions of years ago, some of them got tired of sitting at home. Because they had developed spaceships, which allowed them to sit comfortably while exploring other planets, they decided to send some people to Earth. They thought Earth was warmer, because it was nearer the Sun. You see, the Sun is the big central heating system; the furnace of our universe. It is just like we had one furnace for all the houses in Town.

After the Government of Saturn spent several years discussing the idea of sending people to Earth, they decided first to send an unmanned spacecraft with trees and animals. This was a good idea, because trees and animals need each other. The first tree they sent was the Alder, which we now believe is the oldest tree on Earth. Perhaps the reason alders grow in all directions is because they were looking all around when they first came, and then their children thought it was the way to go. Another tree they sent was the Juniper; they always face the East like they are watching for the Sun. Did you ever notice that their tops all point the one way. Besides that, it has to be a foreign tree because it is the only deciduous tree I know which drops its needles every fall.

Next they sent the dinosaurs; mainly because they wanted to get rid of them, and they landed in what is now China. So the legend has grown about the Dragon, which is still remembered and celebrated in China. Of course, dinosaurs wandered to other places but after a long while they died off because they really weren't suited to life on Earth.

Monkeys were sent next, because they are something like us, and they landed in Africa. There followed other animals, like snakes, and they wiggled their way all over the Earth, except Newfoundland and Ireland. Later some Saturn people came and set up a colony. As long as they could keep in touch by spaceship and radio, everything worked fine. Soon people from other planets like Saturn learned about their experiment and sent numbers of their people. So today we have Chinese, Hindu, Negro and White. Because many of these people got mixed up during the many wars and invasions, there are variations amongst the original races. But we won't worry about that because it doesn't matter anymore. Except for their colour, they are the same as the rest of us.

There are still people on Saturn who are related to some of us, although most of us don't know it. At some stage, long ago and for whatever reason, we lost contact with our ancestors on other planets. They were farther advanced, and still keep records and teach the history of the 'Earth Experiment' to their children. Perhaps they want to make contact with us; but we are not yet far enough advanced to call them; and they are sensitive enough not to cause undue alarm.

One day, about sixty years ago, a man on Saturn decided he would try to contact his distant relative on Earth by transmitting a 'thought'. His name was 'Conseat', because he was one of those who sat all the time. He was conceited enough to believe he could transmit his thoughts many millions of miles (or kilometres, if you like) to a little boy on earth. So for several weeks he concentrated on one distant relative, named Tom, whom he believed from his records would be smart enough to receive the thought. Perhaps you don't realize it, but we all have things in our 'genes', our makeup, which have been hidden for years. It takes something to bring it out; just like turning on a switch.

Tom used to lie on his back in the summer time and watch the clouds drifting. He'd watch the moon, and the many stars and wonder what they were all about. One evening he was sitting on the back step looking at the sky. He picked out Venus, the evening star, and later the Big Dipper and the Pole Star. Although he didn't know it, this was a year when several planets were more visible to earthlings. Saturn was also visible as you looked in a slanted way down from the moon. For some reason he felt uneasy; something was nagging at him, and he couldn't take his eyes off the stars. After he went to bed he kept staring at the stars; he almost went to sleep with his eyes open.

For the next several nights he had the same feeling; like someone was forcing him to look. One night, when he was staring out the bedroom window, a poem came into his mind. Line for line it came, almost as if he was reading it:

Oh, you bright beacon of the eternal blue;
What are you? Oh! How I wish I knew.
One of God's beacons, shining from on high,
Winking and blinking in the far off sky.
Much must you see; of good and evil done,
By men of earth, who, out of light of sun.
Seek the deep shadows where
Their vilest deeds are done.
Yet you keep looking,
Staring, searching from afar.
Are we in any way connected?
My bright thought, and my star?

Tom fell asleep instantly; feeling warm and comfortable and satisfied. On Saturn, Conseat gave a knowing smile, and turned to study something else. He had made the connection without the benefit of radio, through the more reliable medium of genetically connected thought.

The Gun

Did you ever think about guns? Never mind the technical stuff; although the Chinese invented gunpowder, a dangerous product in their genetic memory, they were not satisfied. First they had fun with it, using it much as we do today for celebrations; fireworks with a useful purpose. Also somewhere in memory was the seed of an idea that it could be harnessed for warfare; so at some other point in time the gun was invented. Now no matter what idea is developed, others start working on it with a view to 'improvement'. We 'progressed' from the primitive flintlock to the ballistic missile, retaining improved versions of all the smaller guns in between.

In any kind of battle, except that between the sexes, the idea is to keep as far away as possible from your enemy but still be able to subdue him. So we 'progressed' from the fist and foot to the knife, sword, spear and gun. In ancient times nets with weights were also used to throw over the enemy in order to subdue him; something like a caplin seine. Perhaps that is the origin of the word 'insane', because surely they became mad when entangled in the net.

Now it takes a lot of nerve to confront an enemy face to face; not many can do it, no matter how well trained they may be. It is much easier, and less risky, to shoot when you can't distinguish his features or, in the case of field guns, ballistic missiles and 'smart bombs', you can't see the enemy at all. There are fewer psychological problems that way, so they say.

Not since the Treaty of Utrecht between Britain and France in 1713 has there been any serious warlike action on the island of Newfoundland. We all know, of course, that there was much naval warfare around the coasts between 1939 and 1945, but no actual skirmishes or battles took place on land in the last 290 years. Even individual shootings have been rare, though guns have been harvesting tools in Newfoundland and Labrador for centuries. Only since the city dwellers and bureaucrats of Canada have taken control of our society have we been made to feel guilty about being gun owners. Perhaps the only protection available to us now is to wave a gun permit at intruders. Now the danger is not from the average citizen but from the police; the protectors of society.

On August 26, 2000, Norman Reid of Little Catalina was shot and killed a few minutes after police arrived on the scene. He came out of his house waving an axe at three policemen who were separated from him by a fence. Reid had a long history of mental difficulties and was personally known to the police.

In Corner Brook police responded to a call about Darryl Power on October 16, 2001. He came out of his mother's house carrying a hammer and two knives. Within ten to fifteen minutes he was shot and killed. Like Norman Reid, Power had a long history of mental illness and was well known to the police.

Both violent deaths are the subject of judicial inquiries whose findings will be made available in due course. There are many convoluted theories seeking to explain, or perhaps justify, what happened in such cases. The most farfetched theory is that mentally disturbed persons such as Reid and Power want the police to kill them; a substitute suicide if you will. Well, it seems difficult to accept that theory, especially in Power's case, where the call for help was made to the local hospital. People wonder where police management are hiding after such tragic incidents; it appears that only the constables are answerable to the public. You may wonder where all this is leading? Well, finally we have come to the real story.

In the winter of 1946-7, I was sitting in the Ranger Force Detachment in Nain listening to a Swiss radio station on short wave. The best reception was at night, and in my loneliness, I used to listen to broadcasts in English from Switzerland, Russia and Germany, depending on what appealed to me. The radio was powered by a six volt wet cell battery, like in a car. I had two, and one was nearly always hooked up to the wind charger at the Trading Post. Those who have lived through that era will recall that radio was the only contact with the outside world between October, and June or July of the following year, depending on ice conditions.

Between 9:30 and 10:00 p.m. there was a loud knock on the door. I knew there must be trouble because night visitors were rare. When I went out a very hysterical woman told me in broken English that Dick Pamak was going to kill her daughter. When I got her calmed down somewhat she said that she was at the house and Dick became very abusive. Now I recognized her as Dick's mother-in-law. She told me that she ran from the house and he told her that if she went to the police he would shoot me too.

Now it is difficult to be calm in the face of such a situation, but I tried to be and assured my visitor I would look after the problem. She was to go home and not raise any alarm. After she left, my mind raced at top speed. I knew Dick Pamak; he was one of the best hunters in Northern Labrador; a crack shot and a dour intimidating person who had no friends. Unlike Caesar's wife, Mrs. Pamak 'was not above reproach'. However, she did not deserve to be killed.

Newfoundland Ranger Detachment Building, Nain, Labrador.

I was there alone; the nearest Ranger was at Hopedale 120 line miles away. The next nearest was at Hebron about 200 miles away across the mountains.

The only travel was by dog team, which could take days, depending on weather and travel conditions. There were no telephones through which I could seek advice, or comfort. While there was a Morse set at the Trading Post, the Marconi Station in Hopedale was closed until morning. If I sought help from the village, others would be put at risk; always assuming, of course, that I could get help in such a situation. I am sure you cannot really understand what went through my panicked mind; it is necessary to live through it to really know.

The Newfoundland Ranger Force came into being in 1935 and was a well trained armed Force from its inception. We wore Smith & Wesson .38 revolvers on ceremonial occasions, during prisoner escort, and when particular circumstances required it. On the face of it this was one of those discretionary situations. But Dick's house was down on the point of the harbour, where the airport now is, and about 200 yards from the village. There was no cover for anyone approaching and Dick had a clear field of fire; a revolver was no good. We were also equipped with a .303 Lee Enfield Rifle, which was used mostly for seal and caribou hunting since there was no supermarket. If I took the rifle, it was an invitation to death as there was no way I could conceal it.

If I didn't go at all, I might as well leave Nain in the morning as no one would ever have any respect for me again; my effectiveness would be gone. Talk about being between a rock and a hard place!

Well, I consulted with myself and decided to go; carrying only my flashlight. As I walked through the village, there was not one light in the houses, but I suspect there were many eyes peering through the windows. Because it was around the Easter period, people had come in from their winter places. It was bright moonlight and it glistened and sparkled on the crusted snow; cold comfort for me.

Photo by Hayward Haynes

Cyril Goodyear in Ranger uniform, Nain, Labrador, 1946.

Now, I have been frightened many times in my life. As a child I experienced fear mainly from my own imagination. Fear sometimes chains the mental and physical in some people. In the rest of us it is a cautionary guide to the mind and the body. In my view, it is important for everyone to experience fear at sometime in their lives; and to learn how to function in spite of it. Only fools ignore fear! As I walked slowly across that endless 'space' of snow in the moonlight, flashing my light all over my body as I hoped he could see I was not armed, my knees knocked with fear. At any moment a shot might come from that lampless house.

Finally, I reached the door and raised my hand to knock. He could easily hear the crunch on my sealskin boots as I approached. Before I could knock, the door was wrenched open and there stood Dick with his .30-.30 pointed at me from the waist in classic Western style. "What you want?" he said. My voice was shrill with fear when I said, "Dick, I didn't come to cause trouble, just to prevent it." We looked at each other for what seemed a long time, then I put out my hand and slowly pushed the rifle barrel aside.

After, we sat on the doorstep in the cold night and talked. His wife was alive, and so was I. As I walked back across the snow that chilling night, in the twilight glow of the moon and thousands of winking stars, I began to understand the processes which lead people to believe that someone or something in some remote way injects new reasoning to cope with unusual circumstances. It can't be a controlling mechanism but, perhaps, some form of guidance system locked in genetic memory. During the rest of my stay in Labrador I never again had any trouble.

Years later Dick Pamak became a Special Constable with the Royal Canadian Mounted Police, and a fine citizen. About twenty years after I left the Labrador and the Police, I went back to Nain as a Provincial Court Judge. It was in August and the RCMP float plane landed in the harbour. Special Constable Dick Pamak rowed out to meet me in a dory. As he rowed me towards the wharf he said, "You never got old." I removed my cap and said, "No, Dick, only up here." A broad grin came across his face; the only time I had ever seen him smile. After Court was over and I was ready to leave, I gave him a plain paper bag containing a bottle of his favourite rum. Great lessons had been learned by both of us, cemented by friendly diplomacy.

Dick Pamak eventually retired from his position with the RCMP, and was succeeded by his son Tom. There was a hostage situation in Nain years later and it was Tom who shot and killed the offender. That tragedy is also a matter of public record.

Retirement was good to Dick and he finally died of natural causes. I hope the same happens to me. Perhaps, if the circumstances and the thinking had been otherwise, Mrs. Pamak, Dick or me, or perhaps all three of us, would have died in 1947.

Unitas Fratrum

Cultures, like races, are no longer pure. From the time the various ethnic groups met, or collided with each other on this earth the strong physical and intellectual urges within each dictated mixture. The dominant genes prevailed and passed on the stronger physical characteristics; and aroused interest in almost everything. Foods, clothing styles, utensils, art and gods were adopted and modified over time. The most open minded were as summed up by Ulysses, "I am a part of all that I have met."

All gods are believed to have lived in, or come from, the skies. That belief endures to this day; some of us wonder where that concept originated! The Greeks, like other ancient civilized cultures, were close to their gods; and even classified them. On the intellectual side they were called Muses. There were nine who were believed to prompt, guide and oversee their particular classification. Euterpe was the goddess of music which, by implication, came to us from the 'heavens'. She obviously had great power and insight, and her influence was passed down through the genetic chains of all races. It endures to this day and still fills the yearning gaps in our minds and souls. Music and 'soul' are seemingly inseparable; each has yet to be fully defined and understood.

In Newfoundland we have an old saying about things we don't understand. "It might be good enough to eat." Well, for years I might have said the same about Unitas Fratrum, had I heard the phrase. I suppose the idea was to have what was then a universal label, because all 'educated' people in Western societies studied Latin. It is so intertwined in our language and culture, like all the others, that we are now barely aware of it.

Imagine my surprise when I landed at Nain in Northern Labrador at the end of World War II to discover that it meant a missionary society; the United Brothers. There were Sisters in this Society too, but they had no place in the official title. The wives of the missionaries were also Sisters; a contradiction in terms. The most significant thing, is that this German religious sect had a Latin name.

Since few in Newfoundland and Labrador knew Latin, the group were known as the Moravians. They had Mission Stations stretching from Makkovik in the south to Hebron in the north. Their headquarters was at Nain.

Perhaps an historical sketch is in order. I won't go into great detail because all the information is available in history books, and on the world-wide-web. It may be important for you to read this first; because, despite the religious background of the early historians, they wrote about themselves for the edification of people who had no way of knowing and assessing what they were doing. Most of us who have a limited purpose, tell it the way we want. It is a human thing, no matter how much we attribute it to divine purpose.

Zeal is the engine that empowers many an organization; some members are more zealous than others.

According to history, the Reformation began at Worms in Germany after Martin Luther nailed his 'thesis' to a door. It really gathered momentum in 1529, after the second diet at Spires, and became one of the many 'times of troubles' in the long history of Christianity. During the periods of mutually disadvantageous persecution, some of the 'Protestants' were granted asylum by Count Zinzendorf on his estates in Moravia. Successor Counts continued to offer protection and the Protestant refugees organized themselves as Unitas Fratrum, with their headquarters in Herrnhut. Over time they became a missionary society with branches in England, the West Indies, Africa, Greenland, Labrador and the United States where they have a following to this day. For centuries they have been called 'Moravians', after their birthplace.

The year 2002 was the 250th anniversary of the permanent settlement of the Moravians in Labrador.* There had been four prior journeys made there, either to explore or establish Mission Stations, beginning in 1752. On that voyage in the *Hope*, Johann Christian Erhardt and his group set up a wooden hut at or near what is now Hopedale on the 31st of July; in fact they called the place Hopedale. In September they sailed farther north seeking natives and hoping to barter for furs and other items. On the 13th Erhardt and five members of the crew went ashore, but never returned. The rest of the group left Labrador on the 20th and returned to England, from which they had set sail. It should be noted that only seven days elapsed from the disappearance of Erhardt and his five companions; nobody went ashore to determine what happened to them.

You may wonder what brought about the connection between the German 'Unitas Fratrum' and England. I would suggest that there were three basic reasons:

1. The fact that England was officially a Protestant State, from the time of Henry VIII;
2. European royalty was interconnected, with strong German ties to British royalty during the period we are exploring. There was also the direct intervention of Count Zinzendorf, who appears to have been the real influence in the sect;
3. Newfoundland and Labrador were part of the British Empire, and travel there had to be sanctioned by the government of the day.

I must digress here for a few moments to explain the use of the name 'Eskimo'. That was the original racial label placed on this particular group by the arrogant whites. It is said to mean 'eaters of raw meat'. True, these people ate some meat raw and also partly cooked; but we eat 'rare' meat which really means the same thing. Perhaps the difference is that they had more meat than us, as our supply was rare. The origin of the word 'Eskimo' is unclear, but we mouth the explanation anyway. They are now called 'Inuit', which means 'the people'.

It is really not strange for ethnic groups to refer to themselves as 'the people'. If this were widely researched it would be found that in earlier times all isolated ethnic groups referred to themselves as 'the people'. Even the highly educated cosmopolitan Jews refer to themselves as 'God's chosen people'. For the limited purpose here I will refer to the natives of Northern Labrador as 'Eskimos'. No stigma attaches to that title, as far as I am concerned.

The school at Nain is called 'Jens Haven' after the founder of the Mission Station there. He was a missionary, having served in Greenland, and was selected to make further voyages to Labrador. Unlike the others, he had the advantage of speaking the Eskimo language to some extent since he served in Greenland for two years. Most people don't realize that, except for some variations in local dialect, the same language is spoken from Greenland to Alaska.

Jens Haven was determined to continue the work begun by Erhardt. He was given approval by Zinzendorf to go to London, where he thought he might hire on as a crew member aboard one of the Hudson's Bay Company ships and travel to Labrador. That attempt was unsuccessful, as the Company jealously guarded their turf. Everything works on personalities, and through connections in England he travelled to Newfoundland and Labrador as a guest of the Royal Navy. He made it to Chateau Bay in Southern Labrador in 1764, and again in 1765. He was accompanied by Christian Lawrence Drachart, amongst others, but had to return to England each autumn. Drachart had lived for years in Greenland and was fluent in Eskimo; he was a great asset. Can you imagine what it is like trying to communicate with people who haven't a clue about your language or culture, nor you theirs?

Haven and Drachart spent the period between their return in 1765 and 1769 trying to organize another expedition. They lived at the Moravian settlement at Fulneck, Yorkshire, and lobbied everyone connected with the government. Now it is no secret that expansionist regimes have actively supported missionary work as an instrument of public policy. But there seems to have been some misgivings about supporting a German dominated organization. While it has not been adequately explained, it appears that Unitas Fratrum had to put together an English partner; the Society for the Furtherance of the Gospel Amongst the Heathen. Imagine all those souls out there unaware of the fact that they were 'lost', and about to be 'saved'.

In any event on May 3, 1769, King George III granted 100,000 acres of land in what is now the Nain area jointly to Unitas Fratrum and the Society for the Furtherance of the Gospel Amongst the Heathen. Zeal and persistence paid off and, after considerable organizational efforts, the *Jersey Packet* sailed to Labrador in 1770 and surveyed several sites before choosing Nain. They returned to England to prepare for the establishment of a permanent Mission there the following year.

Just consider the implications of this grant of land! A mad king in remote England, who had not the foggiest idea about the land and the people, granted 100,000 acres of their land to another bunch of foreigners without the knowledge and consent of the people who had lived there for only the gods know how long!

On August 8, 1771, on the good ship *Amity* they returned, laden with supplies and prefabricated buildings. They officially named the place 'Nain' in a moving religious ceremony. The group was made up of German and English personnel and one of their objectives, aside from saving souls, was to carry on trade with the natives; a sort of self sufficient operation. This trading project was carried on, and jealously guarded, until they finally sold out to the Hudson's Bay Company. They in turn sold their stores to the Government of Newfoundland and Labrador in 1942.

Now I hate to bore you with too much historical dates, but it is important to know that only since 1949 has Newfoundland and Labrador been a part of Canada. Some would even argue that union with Canada was a fatal mistake. There is room for doubt, despite the passing years, since only fifty-one percent voted in favour of the union.

Prior to that we had been a British colony, with all the problems that term includes. In 1854 Newfoundland was granted Responsible Government. Dominion status followed and Newfoundland remained independent, within the Empire, until the world-wide depression began in 1932-3. During that period Newfoundland sought assistance, and a Royal Commission under Lord Amulree came to explore and recommend options.

Following the report of the Amulree Commission and because, like many countries, we were insolvent, the Legislature voted to suspend the Constitution. A Commission governed Newfoundland and Labrador from 1934 until one minute before midnight on March 31st 1949. We enjoyed Dominion status again for one minute, and became the tenth Province of Canada on April 1st.

The Commissioners were all appointed, and were under the supervision of the British Colonial Office. There were three British and three Newfoundland Commissioners, with a British Governor; usually a retired Rear Admiral of the Royal Navy. Actually, absent democracy, they did a pretty good job. They listened to their advisors and, generally speaking, ran their departments well. Innovative civil servants often implemented progressive programs in the colonies that they could never get away with in the entrenched societal systems of their home countries.

One of the many recommendations made by the Amulree Commission was the establishment of an organization which would have a multitude of duties, including policing. They were to be stationed around Newfoundland and Labrador and would report regularly to the Commissioner for Natural Resources, through their Headquarters in St. John's. That recommendation was implemented and the Newfoundland Ranger Force was born.**

At age seventeen, I left home in early 1944 to go to the foreign country of Canada to join the Royal Canadian Air Force. I went there because it was cheaper, and involved less hassle. Fortunately, when Hitler finally heard I was in the war, he committed suicide. Along with many millions, I was very thankful. On returning home I joined the Newfoundland Ranger Force and was posted for a short time to Battle Harbour. While there I met Dorothy Jupp, an English nurse stationed at the Grenfell Mission Hospital at Mary's Harbour. After that I was transferred to Nain. That was the beginning of many unusual experiences, for me at least. It was there I learned of Unitas Fratrum (Moravian Mission) for the first time.

Given the route of the coastal boat, the S.S. *Kyle*, through its many ports of call up to Hopedale, and the *Winifred Lee* from there to Nain, it was about 900 miles to Nain. There were no roads anywhere in Labrador, and few in Newfoundland. All travel was by ship, small boat, or dog team in winter. From the middle of October until about the end of June the following year we never saw anyone from the outside world, except Dr. Tony Paddon from the Grenfell Mission at Northwest River. He made one trip each winter by dog team. The only communication system we had, except for boat mail, was Morse Code equipment at the trading posts. When atmospheric conditions were unfavourable, that didn't work. Nain had seven permanent families, as the population of my district lived principally in the bays or fishing places, and visited Nain for trading and religious purposes. It was isolation that few can comprehend today.

Now you've heard enough history, and it's time to talk of people and their influence on the lives of others. I am going to be very selective in that regard; otherwise this will be meaningless. Reverend Bill Peacock, his wife Doris and baby daughter lived in the fenced Mission compound, as well as Reverend Paul and Mrs. Hettesch. I never knew her first name as she was always referred to as 'Mutte'. Their daughter, Kate, lived with them and ran the Mission Boarding School. Kate was a confirmed spinster, a free spirit, very artistic and a good teacher. Like her parents, she was educated in Germany, and had lived most of her life in Northern Labrador. All were fluent in the Eskimo language. They all lived in substantial houses, and the rest of us lived outside the fence.

Peacock had served in Nain for a time and went back to England. At the outbreak of World War II he returned as Superintendent of the Moravian Missions in Labrador, replacing Hettesch who was now summarily retired. Between the two wars the headquarters of the Unitas Fratrum had been moved

Rev. Paul and Mrs. Hettesch, Nain, Labrador, 1946.

to London. The Hettesches, who were now about seventy, were German and their son Seigfried, was the Missionary at Hebron, the most northerly post. It seems to me that, coupled with the war, this was a situation which would strain any relationship; religious or otherwise. The administration of religion is a political game; some politicians are more accomplished than others as we well know.

Germany and Japan and their allies had been soundly defeated, and much of Europe and Asia was in ruins. There was uncertainty, for the Marshall and

MacArthur plans had not yet been devised. Just think of German people; who had lived in isolation from their home country for many years, and in equal isolation from society in their adopted country, with their mixed loyalties and fears. Would we feel any different? What would be the mix of our emotions? They had no home, only Nain, where the few who lived there were rejoicing in the defeat of Germany. It seemed that no one could get inside their heads or earn their confidence, especially an outsider like me; a policeman and ex-member of the Royal Canadian Air Force.

Here I was in alien surroundings, young and inexperienced and considered by Europeans to be relatively uncultured. The one advantage I had was being young and single, always hungry, and living alone. I used all the diplomatic skills I could muster to scrounge coffee, snacks and meals from the Missionaries and the Trading Post Manager and his wife, Hayward and Selma Haynes. All were very good to me; but the Hettesches were especially kind and as I walked the tightrope between the personalities in my naive way, they seemed to take me under their wing. Perhaps the strain of the war and their social, mental and actual isolation had a large influence; but then, I've always gone out of my way to deal with people as I find them.

They taught me quite a bit, as have everyone I have met, and I learned a lot of history of the Mission, Germany and Europe in general. It was an interesting time in many ways, and even awakened an interest in music. The Hettesches always had an afternoon nap, and I would sometimes drop in for tea and cookies for 'Mutte' was a fabulous cook. After a while, perhaps because they ran out of things to talk about, they would ask me if I wanted to listen to some music. What could I say? Here was an uncouth kid from Deer Lake, whose only musical knowledge was western songs and hymns. True, I met a girl when I was doing my basic training in Toronto and she took me to the Toronto Symphony twice; but I was more interested in her than I was in music.

In any event, on that old wind-up phonograph with the scratchy needles, I listened dutifully to Wagner, Handel, Liszt, and a host of others. They had quite a collection, and would explain the operas and the lives of the com-

Author's photo

Kate Hettesch's Retirement Home, Nain, Labrador.

posers. Gradually I got to know and like much of it with the result that, in my second year when I got a radio, I used to sit up half the night to listen to music from London, Berne and Moscow on short wave. Over the years I learned to select and like many classes of music; without those sessions in Nain it might not have happened.

The Reverend 'Paul' was a very versatile man, with a bit of training and experience in everything. One winter George Rich, the son of Chief Joe of the Davis Inlet band of Nascopi Indians, accidently shot himself in the little finger; I've forgotten which hand. Old Shinapeo brought him to Nain for treatment. Reverend Hettesch called on me and asked me to help him with the operation. His bag of surgical tools and the chloroform mask were impressive. He issued all the instructions and I administered the anesthetic. He did that operation in his study. Peeling back the flesh from the shattered bone, he removed the finger at the last joint and sutured the flesh. George stayed with me for a few days until it was certain he was going to be alright. I saw him many times after that and you could hardly tell he ever had a little finger on that hand. I learned to like and admire the Hettesches, especially the old man.

I have many things to help me remember Labrador. One of them is a Liturgy and Hymn Book given to me by Reverend Peacock. It is in the Eskimo language, compiled, translated and published in Germany in 1912. Some of the words have as many as 22 letters; a complete sentence in German or English. The 'Vorwort' is dated April 23rd. What a coincidence; that happens to be my birthday.

How cultures merge, as we have discussed before! The first stage is food and useful implements. There follows the adoption and modification of words. It is an ever changing process, and only stagnant cultures fear it. Always, art and music intermingle. A classic example, aided by genetics, is the ability of the Eskimo people to adopt and excel in playing musical instruments. For example, the first church organ was presented to the Nain congregation by the people of Herrnhut around 1824 and was played with great skill by local persons. When I was there, Nain had a brass band, as did Hopedale. Except when the instruments froze up during outdoor ceremonies, the music was quite good. I remember quite well going to Easter services and hearing the choir sing the 'Messiah' in their own language. While at the time I was not the best judge of musical performances; it was most impressive.

After I left Labrador and moved on to many places and jobs, I kind of lost track of the family; as we often do. There is not much point in regretting it now; better to remember the good things about that friendship. Reverend Paul and Mrs. Hettesch eventually retired to Bethlehem, Pennsylvania, the American Headquarters of the Moravians. They passed away some years ago, exiles in another alien country, leaving a rich legacy. Kate taught for a number of years and retired in Nain. She also moved to Bethlehem some years later, where she too joined her parents.

In 1967 I went back to Nain as a member of the Provincial Court. We had moved to Goose Bay, and I went regularly to the coast on circuit. Kate had bought a retirement house and was busy doing all kinds of things. She had not lost her energy, sense of humour, or her person skills.

Dorothy Jupp was also there as Chief of the Grenfell Nursing Station. In the intervening years they had taken over the medical services throughout central and coastal Labrador. Kate and Jupp were good friends, and it was a pleasure to visit with them after the court sessions were over. Kate regularly visited Shirley and I at Goose Bay, and later when we moved on to other places.

When I returned to Nain I was amazed at the changes. We always tend to expect things to stay the same, except where we are. Since 1771 Nain had grown from a nomadic meeting place to an incorporated town of over 1,000 people. This had happened through a combination of many things. The administrators of church and state always believe it is better to have people within hearing distance of the church bell, and within sight of the bureaucracy. In Newfoundland and Labrador we have gone through several periods of 'resettlement'. It was a smaller version of 'the great leap forward' and the result has been disastrous. Resettlement should be a personal choice, based on opportunity of whatever kind. Motivation is a very complicated thing in human beings.

While roads and airports were still lacking, there was a regular 'bushline' air service. Coastal boat service had improved with new boats and docks, and mail service was year round. Dial telephones were everywhere, and not long after there followed satellite television. The Labrador Inuit Association had been formed and were becoming a power on the coast, as they should be.

It became almost a ritual; whenever I was staying over at Nain I would drop into Kate's before supper. She would lock the door and break out two fine china cups, and we would have a drink or two. Anyone looking through the windows would be sure we were drinking tea. Siegfried, her brother, was now the Missionary at Nain. He would come by occasionally. Kate would unlock the door and I would say, "How are you, Sieg?" He would invariably reply, "I've got problems, problems—."

"Get a cup and have a drink Sieg," Kate would interject. "Your problems will go away." So Siegfried would sit down and we would have a great yarn.

Over time I would be invited for supper, on alternate trips, at Kate's or the Nursing Station. The three of us would have a good meal and talk about old times; shrinking time and space. I never lost the art of scrounging meals. Jupp was a good nurse, widely travelled and very knowledgeable. She was very quiet, not boisterous like Kate, but a good friend. We all looked forward to those visits; not everyone can recover the past so easily!

One evening in September, after a lengthy court session, I was invited to the Nursing Station. During the meal Kate and Jupp were joking about dessert. I tried not to be too curious because it would spoil their fun. Finally the dessert arrived; three large bowls with one strawberry and a blob of canned cream in each. It was their total crop of strawberries from their garden that year. I've been musing about these events ever since!

* For more details see "Periodical Accounts" http://www.mun.ca/rels/morav/texts/ship.html AND http://www.mun.ca/rels/morav/texts/brethren.html as well as other historical material.

** See *History of the Newfoundland Ranger Force*, by Harold Horwood.

The Hoop Theory

When you think about it, almost everything is a 'closed circuit system'. To put it in the simplest terms, the biggest example is the Earth. It rotates around the sun, with one half in alternate darkness. Heat and light, darkness and cool; clouds form to filter the sun and ultimately provide rain and snow to water the earth. Up goes the moisture and then comes back down again as rain and snow. Trees and plants grow and provide food, shelter, oxygen and other things necessary to sustain life. In this continuous recycling process all things live, perform, adapt, excrete, fertilize, die and are reborn in successive forms; it is a seemingly endless process. It is not automatic, except in the general sense, and the process varies in each individual case. All life, within its genetic limits, takes on individual characteristics. For example, a spruce tree can be recognized because of its peculiar shape and size, resulting from the effects of wind, snow, water, animals and man. Each species has a degree of individuality which develops, thankfully, within the overall system and allows some limited choices to be made

This is a rather simplistic explanation, and there is nothing really new about it; just put in a different way. While we cannot know whether trees and plants have the capacity to make choices, because we do not speak their language and they are not mobile of themselves, except as seeds carried by the wind, water and animals; we do know about animals. Over the centuries we have learned to communicate with many species, and they with us as individuals themselves; consider your horse, dog or cat.

But what is the basis of all this communication with other species and our own? Of course it is the brain you say! The brain, the mind, the intellect or whatever you wish to call it. But it really can't be a blank organism, can it, waiting to be turned on like a computer. Or maybe it is; for the computer is already programmed and ready to be manipulated, as is the brain. In the plant world the seed is the brain. It is already programmed and knowing what to do when conditions are right. So each seed or brain, of whatever kind, has an archival or genetic memory and perhaps like everything around us, some are more complete and more sophisticated than others. Who knows but that may explain many of the great discoveries over time. For example, Leonardo da Vinci (1452-1519) did detailed drawings of a submarine and a helicopter before anyone had any concept of what they were. While the submarine was 'invented' in the 19th. century, the helicopter was not 'invented' until the late twentieth century. Albert Einstein, 1879-1955, and his 'theory of relativity' may have a similar explanation.

Language is another example: ethnic origin, i.e. race, is a major determinate of language. While persons of one race can learn several languages, it seems that genetic memory has a major effect; again the 'seed' may be the key. Who knows but that the 'origin of the species' may not be as simple as some scientific and religious groups may think. No one has adequately explained race, colour and language. Perhaps our forebearers came from different places in the universe with similar atmospheric, climatic and other conditions. Maybe 'multi-speakers' were ambassadors who dealt with people on other planets. People we know who 'have an ear for language' may be genetically connected with people beyond Earth. It may be that in time, the secrets of genetic memory will be unlocked through a combination of 'prompted' thought and technological advances; especially through space exploration.

Let us look at the closed circuit system of human decision making and behavior. Knowing as little as we do now, our lives resemble a series of rotating circles, or hoops, which become progressively smaller and reduce ultimately down to a spot in the innermost centre. After all, the circle or ellipse is common in all aspects of the universe. Just visualize the planet Saturn with its surrounding rings.

Before conception we are a nebulous unfertilized seed. We are only a possibility and not even on the outer hoop. When our parents select each other, we are a probability contained in two genetically programmed seeds. When we are born, in theory we are on the outer hoop going round in circles.

The moment we are born our total freedom is curtailed to some extent; prior to that the permutations were almost endless. Depending on who our parents are, i.e. race, social status, occupation, religion, physical condition, location on earth, etc., our freedom of choice is already diminished. For example, as soon as we begin to attend school we move to another hoop where we circulate until graduation. The end result of freedom of choice, whether our parents' or ours, is to limit choice.

Whatever the next choice, whether university or work, we move to the next smaller hoop. We circle endlessly on it until we graduate, or choose a girl or boy friend, or both and begin to work. Moving to the other hoop we marry; now we can no longer play the field, freedom of choice is again limited; depending on many circumstances. Children are born to us, again limiting our freedom to choose. If we decide, or because of reasons of health, age, finances, location or a host of other reasons end up in the same occupation, choices are again limited.

Retirement moves us to another hoop, and increasing age and infirmity again moves us ever inward to a still smaller hoop. Our spouse passes on and finally, we move to that last spot in the centre and die. Undoubtedly you can think of numerous examples which can be inserted in this theory. But the facts are clear; we live in a closed circuit system, always subject to 'the hoop theory' or in more intellectual terms, 'the theory of diminishing freedom'.

Consider the universe; it is also a 'closed circuit system', albeit much larger than Earth which is merely a part of our galaxy, which again is merely a part of the universe. Time and distance only make it seem endless to our small form of life. Because of the vast distances, almost beyond our comprehension, we have coined the phrase 'alien world'. Anything that is 'foreign' to us, i.e. beyond our knowledge and experience, is alien. We have used the word to describe human beings who were not born in our country as well as imaginary beings from other planets in the galaxy and universe.

Stonehenge, Salisbury Plain, HK, 1999.
Author's photos.

How did this come about, this reference to 'aliens' from outer space? Both the Biblical account of creation and the 'big bang' theory, as well as the theory of evolution seem to exclude such 'aliens' from conventional wisdom. Perhaps genetic memory is the answer, and it may be prompted as in the mythical case of Conseat on Saturn. Surely it did not come about as a result of mere speculation arising from our own conscious brains; they produced the 'Biblical', 'big bang' and 'evolution' theories.

Why should we call anyone alien? Is a black, brown, yellow or white person alien to any and all of the others? Is it conceivable and logical that people from outer space, believed to visit occasionally in 'flying saucers', are any different from the races which inhabit earth? Even *Star Wars* pursues the theme that, despite some physical differences, the inhabitants of other planets have much in common with humans. On Earth, different races have distinctive eyes, noses, hair and other noticeable characteristics. Could this be an indirect means of educating earthlings to prepare for the day when real contact will be made again? With the space programs of the United States and its partners it may become a two way street. After all, in March 2002, the thirty year old Pioneer 10 sent a signal back to earth from a distance of over seven billion miles. The time lapse for the signal was twenty-three minutes. Just think about the ease with which a superior civilization could communicate and travel.

When you think about it, there is an element of truth in everything we hear and think. Myths have circulated for thousands of years, perhaps based on some real fact which lost its realism in the oral history which changed because of the passage of time and the lack of physical experience in direct human contact. Who knows but that the mythical Irish 'Leprechauns', a race of smaller people, did exist and have been kept alive in genetic memory and perpetuated in mythology?

Perhaps, with ever increasing knowledge resulting from ever widening space exploration, the Hoop Theory will be reversed for us intellectually, and we will begin at the centre and move to hoops of ever increasing size. In genetics the intellectual and physical are inseparable; the immortality of each cannot survive without the other. Conseat and his counterparts, rather than conceit, may help us. As it says in the Bible, in the Gospel of St. John. Chapter 8, verse 32, "And ye shall know the truth, and the truth shall make you free."

Nearer to Mars

By the time Sarah was eleven years old she had read everything she could about outer space. She was obsessed by it and never tired of getting her Uncle Cy to tell about how he met Major Yuri Gagarin, the Russian cosmonaut who was said to be the first man in space. He told her over and over again about when Gagarin came to Nova Scotia as the guest of Cyrus Eaton in August, 1961, during the Cold War.

Gagarin, who was an officer in the Soviet Air Force, was accepted as a cosmonaut trainee in 1959 at the base in Zvezdniy, Gorodok. Not quite two years later, the record shows that on April 12, 1961, Major Gagarin made a 108 minute orbit of the earth having blasted off on the nose of Vostok 1.

Eaton was born at Pugwash, Nova Scotia. He moved to Cleveland, Ohio in the United States and became a multi-millionaire steel maker. Mr. Eaton was a known Communist sympathizer, and he and his family moved freely between the United States and the Soviet Union. His step-daughter spoke fluent Russian.

Uncle Cy was living in Halifax at the time and was in charge of the RCMP Criminal Investigation Section for the Province. As he explained to Sarah, he often supplied men on security jobs, and frequently went himself. Since Gagarin's visit was unofficial, i.e. he was not there as guest of the Federal Government, it was vitally important that nothing go wrong which would embarrass either country. Security was very tight, both visible and otherwise. The Security and Intelligence Branch had a large number of men on the fringes who were not accredited to the visiting party, but kept a watchful eye on everyone especially the KGB agents who travelled with Gagarin. It might interest you to know that in those days the S&I, as it was called, was a branch of the RCMP. The spy agency now is a civilian agency, although there are probably some ex-RCMP members in it. Uncle Cy was told that the Soviet Army general in charge of Gagarin's party was actually a KGB general, a member of the secret police.

When the Soviet party landed at Halifax Airport on August 5, there were brief statements to the Press by the Soviet Ambassador to Canada and Cyrus Eaton. The party then left for Deep Cove, near Blandford, where Mr. Eaton had a farm stocked with prize cattle. They all toured the farm, and that night there was a big banquet which Uncle Cy attended. Of course he was at the end of the last table; Uri Gagarin was the celebrity. The main dish was roast leg of lamb, with all the trimmings. It was really interesting to see how Gagarin was handled; like a puppet.

The next day the large party drove up to Pugwash. Just in case you don't know, that is up near Amherst close to the New Brunswick border. Mr. Eaton had a large estate there where he often entertained prominent people at his 'Thinkers Conferences'. There was another big dinner that night with all kinds of fish dishes. Uncle Cy enjoyed that part of the job. At the Press Conference the Soviet Ambassador, the General, Mr. Eaton and Uri Gagarin all spoke. Interpreters made sure everybody understood what was said. There were selected news reporters from all over the world; what a propaganda victory for the Soviets.

Uncle Cy took particular notice of the fact that when technical questions were put to Gagarin, it was the General who answered. It was so obvious that they didn't trust Gagarin, or he didn't know! There was extreme paranoia in both the East and the West. Uncle Cy always said that, while the Soviets undoubtedly put the first man in space, it wasn't Uri Gagarin. Perhaps the first Cosmonaut died before being recovered. It was rumoured for years that the son of the Soviet aircraft designer, Illushin, was the first man in space. He was said to have died in an unfortunate space accident. On the other hand, the Soviets were very open about the death of Vladimir Komarov. He also did several orbits of the Earth, but died on April 24, 1976 during reentry when the parachute of the reentry vehicle tangled.

Yuri was a very pleasant looking man; all personality. He looked and acted like a movie star; an advertiser's dream.

The next day, August 6, the party returned to Halifax Airport where they were supposed to leave for Moscow. But there was a delay; the Ambassador was on the phone to Moscow, then Mr. Eaton and the General. The phone lines were tapped and Uncle Cy and others knew something unusual was about to happen. They announced a delay in departing, saying that their plane had mechanical trouble. But it was confirmed this was a ruse when Cyrus Eaton spoke openly in English to someone in Moscow.

Now shortly after Mr. Eaton spoke to Moscow, Quent Wenaus who was on the security detail with

Uncle Cy, went to the washroom in the airport. As he was standing there he looked to his right and there was Cyrus Eaton. Quent, who was a very outgoing person, changed hands and said, "Nice to meet you Mr. Eaton, I'm Quent Wenaus." They shook hands and left the washroom.

What really happened was that the Soviets had another man in space, Major Gherman Titov, and they were arguing whether the effect on world opinion would be greater if Gagarin was in Russia or North America when Titov landed. Eaton and the General argued that Garagin should be in Canada at the time of the landing, and should then rush home to congratulate Titov. Their argument failed and Garagin left shortly thereafter to be on hand when Titov was brought back to earth.

Many people on the ground in Halifax sneered that the Russians couldn't get their plane off the ground, even though they had launched two men in space. But really it was a scam; they knew Titov was up there and they had to create a reason for delay while their bosses in the Kremlin decided the best strategy for their propaganda war.

Gagarin became a great celebrity, travelling the world as an example of Soviet superiority. He is reported to have rejoined the space program but was killed in a training flight on March 27, 1968. He is buried near the Kremlin wall in Moscow, a victim of human time and space.

Sarah was fascinated with anything to do about flight and space. She watched the birds and read about them. Her father, Uncle Jim, certainly helped increase her interest; especially about crows. But she had more interest in aggressive birds like the osprey, hawk and the eagle. There was some vague feeling inside her, which she could not explain, when she watched those noble birds. It was particularly strong the day they were travelling on the boat to Harbour Deep, when they watched a bald eagle soaring along the edge of the cliffs.

In school, during science class, Sarah could tell them that the moon is a satellite of Earth which revolves around it once every twenty-nine and a half days, and shines at night by reflecting the sun's rays. It was a great thrill for her to watch the science programs about Neil Armstrong and Buzz Aldrin landing on the moon. But, for some strange reason, she was really interested in Mars. She would tell you it was known as the 'Red Planet', and that the Romans believed that Mars was the 'God of War'. She followed all the space news about the Mars 'Lander' and the belief of scientists that Mars may have once supported life like ours on Earth.

One day she said to Uncle Cy, "I'd like to climb a mountain."

"What for?" he asked.

"Well, I'd just like to climb one." she said.

"Ok," he replied, "If the weather is fine on Saturday, and if you're free, we'll do it. We'll climb Gros Morne in the National Park."

On Friday, after school, she collected her hiking gear and her mother drove her over to spend the night with Aunt Shirl and Uncle Cy. They checked out the gear; boots, spare socks turned inside out because they're softer, sweater, wind jacket, hat, gloves and sun glasses. Uncle Cy packed lunch; four big sandwiches, oranges, pop and Mars bars. He put two large plastic bottles of water in the freezer. "What is that for?" asked Sarah. "It is a long climb to the top," he said, "and we'll be very thirsty. As the ice melts on the way up we'll have lots of cold water."

Uncle Cy put his camera, field glasses, and cell phone in his pack. The cell phone was put in a hard plastic box, so that it could stand the banging about. He checked to make sure his compass was in the pocket, because up on Gros Morne when the mist comes down you lose all sense of direction.

"Now then, little mountain climber, off to bed because we get up at five o'clock tomorrow morning."

"Five o'clock!" Sarah exclaimed. "Why so early?"

"Well, the last part of the climb is up through the gorge to the top. If it's hot tomorrow, we want to go up in the shade of the rock wall. We won't have to work so hard and we can take our time up on top and won't have to rush back like we would if we left here later."

"Ok," she said, and went to bed.

Five o'clock saw them having breakfast, because both woke early enough to see if the day would be suitable. There was a mist over the White Hills, but the sun was bright on the Topsails to the east. They hopped into the Jeep and half an hour later were in the parking lot at Deer Arm, at sea level. Uncle Cy strapped on his pack and he and Sarah walked in the ever-rising trail to the base of Gros Morne. It took them over an hour, so they sat for a few minutes looking across the small valley and up the mountain. The steep gorge ran up the mountain on the southeast side, and they could see that the right hand side of it was in the shade.

They crossed the little valley and started up the boulder-strewn gorge. It was hard going and Sarah was glad she brought her gloves as she scrambled and hauled herself up the mountain. Lots of times her Uncle had to help her over, and around the boulders. Broken jagged rocks were everywhere. Every now and then Uncle Cy passed her the bottle of ice water. As fast as they drank, it ran out in sweat; Sarah thought she would never make it.

Finally, after more than an hour and a half, they found the going easier and moved up the slopes to the summit. There were shrubs and coarse grass and wild flowers here and there. Suddenly they saw two arctic hares feeding, just up a little gully. The hares stopped and looked at them and went back to their breakfast. Sarah whispered, "My, aren't they big rabbits."

"They're arctic hares," Uncle Cy said. "They must weigh ten pounds."

"What would that be in kilograms?" asked Sarah.

"I don't know; we didn't learn that when I went to school."

A little farther on several ptarmigan were feeding. They just moved out of the way because they couldn't believe anyone on the mountain would hurt them. The top of Gros Morne is covered with rusty coloured rocks and boulders. From the highway the top appears to be smooth, but not when you get there. "Look Uncle Cy, the top of the mountain looks like we must be on the moon," Sarah said.

"These are some of the oldest rocks in the world," said Uncle Cy. "After all, this area is a World Heritage Site you know."

When they reached the summit they saw a cairn, and rock wall nearby. Uncle Cy pulled Sarah's sweater and wind jacket out of the pack, along with his own. They sat comfortably in the shelter of the rocks out of the wind. He handed her the cell phone, "Call your mother, just punch 03." When Sarah's mother answered she said; "You made it, what does it look like?"

"Mom," Sarah said, "I can see all over the world! To the west there's Forteau in Labrador across the Gulf; I can see Portland Head to the North and the rusty Tablelands to the south, but I can't see Deer Lake because of the mountains."

"My, how wonderful!" said her mother. "How do you feel?"

"I feel very close to Mars," said Sarah.

They took their time coming down; ate two lunches and drank lots of pop and water. The view from the north rim, looking down into the gorge and lake, was awesome. Scudding clouds made strange patterns on the waves, way down in the Gulf. As they spiraled down the other trail off the mountain they saw four caribou feeding in the valley. It was a satisfying day, and Sarah slept soundly that night; not even dreaming about Mars.

The *Pole Star*

"Tell me a story Uncle Cy," Sarah said. He was sitting by the back door, under the canopy, watching the robins in the garden. While they didn't come right up to him, those robins were nesting under the patio deck, and moved about the garden without fear; they knew a friend when they saw one. Sarah put down his cup of tea and her Coke and sat across from him. The request for stories were more frequent these days. Sarah found it a lot easier than reading; and more interesting. She knew he would always start the story in an indirect way and that the point would come out later on. Sometimes he just talked, as older people do, while trying to focus on a suitable story out of his experience.

"Now Sarah," he said, after a sip of tea, "when you go to the supermarket, do you really think about what your mother and you buy? Where do those apples come from, and who picked them? Did the picker ever get a chance to eat one? I used to think a lot about apples when I was a boy, though I don't think as much about them lately. We used to get apples only once in a while, mostly at Christmas. You see, not only were we poor, but the transportation system wasn't as good as now. You can get grapes from California in a few days now. Then, most apples were available only in the fall because we didn't have the means to store them."

"Goodyear Humber Stores in Deer Lake used to keep barrels of them in their basement. Now it wasn't a concrete basement, just boarded up around the foundation. On frosty nights I used to walk up and down past the store just to smell the apples. You might have a job to believe that, because now things are so plentiful."

Sarah searched her uncle's face to see if he was joking. She knew he wasn't because he always had that crooked grin when he joked. "I often wonder where the kiwis and the pineapple come from," she said.

"When you go into the store now, mostly what you see is cut and packaged," continued Uncle Cy. "Most people never think of a cow or bull when they see a steak; or a fish when they see those colourful salmon steaks. Because someone else does all the work we just accept things as they are. Even the animal rights people don't have the same reaction when they go shopping; everything is NORMAL in the supermarket. It's just like when we wear leather shoes or jackets; they came that way!"

"Now I'll tell you the story of the *Pole Star*. Not the real Pole Star up in the sky, but about sealing ships. There were several others, including the *Arctic Sealer*, whose captain was Skipper Jim Jillett from Twillingate and the *North Star VI* under Captain William Moss of Carmanville."

"Is it an old time story Uncle Cy?"

"In a way. But it is also true, and anyone who is interested can read it in the newspapers of that time and in the Royal Canadian Mounted Police files in Halifax. It happened in 1962 out in the Gulf of St.

Lawrence, roughly between Nova Scotia and Newfoundland."

"I know," she said, "Out where we cross on the ferry between Port aux Basques and North Sydney."

"That's right, roughly in that area and also off Prince Edward Island and the Madeleine Islands."

"You know from reading the history of Newfoundland and Labrador in school that sealing was a big industry. We were involved in the seal harvest on a commercial basis for over 200 years. While the catch varied from year to year, it was not unusual for the total to be over half a million. One of the most successful sealing captains was Abram Kean. People say that during his career he brought in over a million seals. He was a Millionaire in Seals. In fact, on April 23, 'my birthday', 1934 a ceremony took place at Bowring Brothers in St. John's. Captain Kean was presented with an award and cheque commemorating his landing of over 1,000,000 seals during his career as a sealing captain."

"If you want to see seals close up, you can visit the Marine Centre at Logy Bay, near St. John's. But in any case you can see them almost anywhere around the coast in the spring. I saw two out in front of a house in Jackson's Arm last spring. The house was right on the harbour and those seals just lay there suntanning just like you do in Florida. I didn't notice what kind of bathing suits they had on."

"Where do the seals come from?" asked Sarah. "Are they Newfoundlanders?"

Uncle Cy laughed. "Some are Newfoundlanders, but most of them are tourists who come down from Greenland and other places up north. They drift down on the ice in the spring and have their babies in the warmer places, then they swim back again. Kind of crazy, isn't it? But then, when you look at those fuzzy whitecoats with the big watery eyes you forget about that. The babies grow very fast because the milk they drink is over fifty per cent butter fat. Just think how fast you would grow on that milk. Our strongest cows milk is only eight percent.

"What do they eat?"

"Our fish," said Uncle Cy. "It's not packaged like you get in the supermarket, but they eat millions of pounds of fish. Along with over-fishing by foreigners, seals are responsible for the shortage of fish around the coast of Newfoundland and Labrador."

"Seals have surnames like people. Some are called Harps because they have a little brown patch on their sides which looks like the harps angels play. Another family is called Hoods; not because they are crooks, although they are pretty nasty sometimes. When they get mad their heads blow out like a parka hood. Those are the two main families of seals which come down from the arctic. Local seals, like Greys or Rangers, hang around the bays and often go up into the rivers after salmon and trout. Most people who talk about why salmon are no longer as plentiful don't mention seals as being part of the problem. Seals kill fish all the time and are seldom punished."

"Anyway," said Uncle Cy, seeing Sarah squirm a little. "Let's get back to the main story. One night in March 1962, when we lived in Halifax, I got a call from the commanding officer, Assistant Commissioner Tony McKinnon of the RCMP. He asked me to come down to his house in the south end of the city. This was unusual, as I had never been in his home before, though I saw him almost every day at the Headquarters Building on Hollis Street. When I got there Mrs. McKinnon served me a cup of coffee. Old Tony, as we used to call him behind his back, used to stutter and, except when he was angry, it took a long time to get to the point. He said, "You've heard the news reports about the sealing ships, and how someone is supposed to be stealing the pelts?" "Yes," I replied, "It could be a nasty situation, but what has it got to do with me?"

"Well," he said, "I had a call from the Commissioner in Ottawa, who had a call from the Minister of Foreign Affairs. They are very nervous, as there are several Russian ships out there also, and they are afraid there might be an embarrassing international incident. Someone is stealing the seal pelts from the ships using helicopters and bringing them ashore. The Ministers of Justice of New Brunswick, Nova Scotia, Newfoundland and Prince Edward Island all say that this is taking place in international waters, and there's nothing they can do. It has to be stopped and that is where you come in."

"I looked at him, aghast." Uncle Cy said. "How am I going to do that, Sir?"

"Well, I don't know, but you are a Newfoundlander, you lived up in Labrador, and your people used to be sealers years ago. You will figure something out. I want you the catch the morning plane to Charlottetown, because the helicopters are bringing the pelts ashore in PEI. That is now the closest place to the sealing ships. I'll call the Commanding Officer there and tell him you have carte blanche authority. If you have any trouble, call me."

"Now Old Tony was a formidable man, and the highest ranking RCMP officer in the Atlantic region. I knew that as long as I didn't do anything stupid he would back me."

"When I got home and told Aunt Shirl, she shrugged and said she was sure I'd figure something out. At the time I was in charge of the Criminal Investigation Squad for the Province of Nova Scotia and we had a lot of important investigations on the go. I phoned Quent Wenaus, the guy who met Cyrus Eaton in the washroom when Uri Gagarin was in Halifax, and we organized the work in Nova Scotia for the next couple of weeks."

"Quent drove me to the airport the next morning, and we talked about the case. He told me that if he was assigned to that job he wouldn't know what to do. I told him we were in the same boat; I didn't have a clue but would play it by ear. In those days we didn't try to find excuses for not doing things, we just kept at it."

"My Gosh, Uncle Cy, what a situation to be in. How did you know what to do?"

"I didn't," I said with a grin. "You've watched mysteries on TV and at the movies. The detectives always start out knowing very little. They ask questions, make mistakes and get fooled, but with a lot of luck most of the crimes get solved. Your Uncle is a genius, of course." "Yes, I know that," she said, with a mischievous laugh.

"When I got to Charlottetown I went to Headquarters and checked in with the Commanding Officer. He didn't seem too pleased to have an outsider come in, but there wasn't much he could do about it. The Charlottetown Motel was across the street, so I checked in there. What a lucky day! I discovered that the helicopter mechanic from the group that was stealing the seals was staying there. I went to his room to see him. There he was, surrounded by beer and liquor bottles, having a drink of rum. He was half-slewed, as they say in Wesleyville. I was in plain clothes, very friendly, and before long I had the whole story. You see, it never pays to be the big smart-alex detective."

"He told me, between drinks which I didn't share, that Dr. Marc Arsenault of Grindstone, Madeleine Islands owned a seal processing plant there. For years they used to get seals like everyone else using boats. But the good Doctor had a bright idea; they would take their hunters out by helicopter and ferry the seal pelts back in. In that way they would have all the seals they wanted before the ships could break through the drift ice to get at the herd. The mechanic said that Dr. Arsenault had studied the ice reports going back about 100 years. With the prevailing winds and the ocean currents the drift ice nearly always moved close to the Madeleine Islands. He cut a deal with a Mr. Connors of Montreal, who owned helicopters, to share in the profits and they began their hunt in early March."

"As the drift ice with thousands of seals moved farther away from their base, they found that they could make few trips and that their novel idea wasn't going to pay. You see the winds were different from previous years. There wasn't time enough to drop off the hunters, kill the seals and ferry them back to shore. While they didn't intend to be crooked in the beginning, as far as we could find out, they had to make a decision or the whole thing would be a flop."

"So, what did they do? said Sarah.

"Well, I got to tell you how the sealing ships operate first, so that you can understand. The ships, like the *Pole Star*, are icebreakers and they push their way in through the drift ice until they see a large patch of seals. Then they heave to and let the men over the side. You got to have a lot of nerve to be a sealer. The men jump down on the moving ice pans and skip from one to the other on the way out to kill the seals. The ocean swell makes the ice go up and down in waves; everything is moving."

"Sarah, can you picture it in your mind? Thirty to forty men out on the moving ice with their gaffs, no life jackets and not all that well dressed."

"What is a gaff?" she asked.

"Well, you know the pole I use with my canoe?" She nodded. "It's like that only there's an iron point and hook on the big end. The men used it, not only to kill the seals, but to help themselves across the ice; it was a safety thing, which is now banned. The government has more concern for seals than it has for people."

"As far as the eye can see, nothing but moving ice covered with the black dots of men and seals. At that time of the year there's not much sun; only fog, rain and snow flurries and ice - ice - ICE. You know how cold the wind is in March and early April, but there's not a doorway to duck into; the only shelter is aboard that distant ship. It makes me shiver, just thinking about it."

"Oh my," Sarah said. "Aren't they afraid?"

"Of course the younger ones are scared to death, the older men cautious, but they cover up their fear by making silly jokes and trying to outdo the other fellow. Sometimes fear is the best safety device. Don't forget though that it was a way of making a living. Most fishermen had no work in the early spring and this gave them extra money."

"When they got into a patch of seals they would club them and skin them on the ice. The fat was always left on the pelt because it makes good oil. You can lay a piece of seal fat down on a board and the oil will run out of it without being heated up. Before people had electricity, seal oil and whale oil were used in lamps for light. That was a long time ago before kerosene oil and white gas. Even I can't remember that far back. I can remember Inuit in Northern Labrador burning seal fat in their stoves. Before that they used it in stone lamps for cooking. The lamp was called a 'kudlik' and was really a hollow stone to hold the seal oil, with a wick made of caribou moss. In later years the refined oil was used in making margarine, paint and other things."

"I know this sounds kind of gruesome, but it is no different than what happens to cattle, pigs, lambs and chickens being processed for steaks and chops. The only difference is you don't see that; but you do see films of the seal hunt. Red blood on white ice really looks terrible; but the reality is that there is no difference in the process, it just makes good fund-raising propaganda for the animal welfare organizations."

"Anyway, when the seals are skinned the front flippers are cut off; that makes two holes in the pelts. When they have fifty to a hundred pelts they cut the ship's initials in the fat of two or three pelts, like *PS* for *Pole Star*, and then they run a cable sling through the flipper holes. Then they put up a flag to mark the piles. The ship's crew hauls out a cable from the ship, sometimes up to a mile long. They hook onto the slings and the ship winches the whole thing back aboard, where they stow the pelts in the ship."

"What happens to all that meat?"

"Well, that's the unfortunate thing, except for the flippers the men take to sell privately, it's all left on the ice."

"What a shame." said Sarah. "There are millions of people around the world going hungry. Isn't there something we can do about that, Uncle Cy?"

"I can tell you there is a good market for seal meat in Newfoundland and Labrador, and perhaps other places, but it really needs a national marketing program. Seal meat is very nutritious, can be cooked numerous ways, and would help millions of hungry people as well as revive the industry. It is really similar to the cattle and meat packing industry, although it is more like the fishing industry; only a bit more dangerous.

"Anyway, back to the story. Now this was ideal for the Arsenault and Connors crews. All they had to do was land the helicopters, hook up the slings and fly away. They landed some at Grindstone on the Madeleine Islands, where they were processed in the plant. As the ice moved south they began to land the seal pelts on the beach at North Rustico, PEI."

"It all began to fall into place. Now I could prove that the seal pelts were stolen from the ships. But the problem was that the thefts took place in international waters where Canada didn't then have any legal right to prosecute. I searched the Criminal Code from cover to cover to find a way the bring them to court. The only section there which might work, was one which made it a criminal offence to bring into Canada property obtained by crime. I don't remember the section number now but it is still there in the Criminal Code, even though the Code has been amended since and the numbers changed. But you had to be able to prove that the crime committed outside Canada would have been a crime if it took place in Canada. That was easy really, because stealing is a crime everywhere."

"I went to the Provincial Court in Charlottetown and got a search warrant so that we could seize the seal pelts for evidence. Then I made an arrangement with a local trucking company to transport the seized pelts to Eastpack Cold Storage plant in Souris. They didn't have much room so I seized only forty tons of seal pelts. Those pelts were getting pretty smelly and greasy now after lying on the beach in the late March and April sun. You see, I could have seized 200 tons or more but the law is that you must take care of what you seize. I took the largest amount that could be stored, just to be on the safe side; it was still a huge seizure."

"Trouble arose when I got a radio call advising that the PEI Minister of Justice wanted to see me. When I went in to see him in Charlottetown he was very angry. You see he didn't like the idea that an investigation was going on in his Province when he had ruled they had no jurisdiction. I carefully explained that I was conducting an investigation for the Federal Government. It's not very pleasant to have a Minister of Justice mad at you. There wasn't much he could say about that so he accused me of breaking the law in PEI by trucking forty tons of seal pelts over the gravel roads from North Rustico to Souris, which were officially closed to traffic. There wasn't much I could say except that I was a stranger to the Island and the owner of the trucking company didn't say anything about the roads being closed. When I told him the name of the owner, he stopped complaining. I learned later that the owner was his friend and political supporter."

"Like the Minister, the RCMP on the Island didn't like having an outsider doing a successful investigation there. They were reporting what I was doing to the Minister. What they couldn't control was the fact that I was reporting regularly to Assistant Commissioner Tony McKinnon."

"Well," Sarah said, "it must have been awful to be caught between all those people."

"Yes, but as you get older you'll find similar situations. The main thing is to try to handle them in a mannerly and diplomatic way so that nobody gets hurt, and you can always come back and deal with those people."

"There was another big problem," said Uncle Cy. "While we would be able to prove that they stole seal pelts and brought them ashore, how could we say they came from a particular ship, or that they didn't kill the seals themselves? There were several ships out there besides the *Pole Star*, and it was necessary to pin down where the pelts came from."

"How could you do that?"

"Well, you see it wasn't easy," said Uncle Cy, rubbing his knuckles on his chest and grinning. "I knew from past experience, and from listening to the tales of old sealers like Skipper Bill Winsor, that the men would always cut the ship's initials in the fat of several pelts in every pile they got ready to be taken to the ship, like I told you earlier. Otherwise there would always be a racket over who owned the pelts."

"It is a fact that not all tissue dies at the same time. When a seal is skinned there is always some hemorrhaging through the fat. It only takes a few minutes to skin a seal on the ice and when the sealer cuts the initials *PS* in the fat, there will always be traces of blood around the cut. Also, as several days pass the outside of the fat oxidizes; that is crusts over. So a person can see that an early cut looks different from one made later."

"I'm only going to talk about the *Pole Star* to make it simpler. When the sealers cut *PS* in the fat, the seals were just dead. Along came the thieves several days later and they cut a stroke on the *P*, turning it into an *R*, and one across the *S*, turning it into an *8*. I could see the difference, but that wasn't good enough, as we would have to prove it scientifically."

"What did you do?" asked Sarah.

"Why, I just phoned Madame Rouen at the Crime Lab at Sackville, New Brunswick and explained the problem to her. I had worked with her before on several cases. She said that if I was right she would not have any trouble proving that the *PS* had been changed to *R8*. So I picked out ten marked seal pelts from the forty tons, put them in the police car and drove them up to Sackville. Had to keep the windows open, because they were beginning to stink; and the grease saturated the trunk. It didn't matter to me because that was a PEI police car."

"Before the investigation was finished I went back to Nova Scotia to interview the crews of the sealing ships. They were docked at Karl Karlson's sealing plant at Blandford, near Hubbards, unloading their catch. You had to hold your nose to walk around the place, but it was really interesting. Everywhere you went on the ships there was seal fat. The hand rails were coated, as was almost everything else. I got statements from the captains and crews, just in case someone decided we could take the matter to court. They treated me like a king aboard the ships because they felt I was the one who had stopped the thefts. What could I say?" said Uncle Cy, again rubbing his knuckles across his chest and grinning.

"Madam Rouen did her tests and issued a report showing that the initials in the fat had been altered, since the P and S had been cut before the two knife cuts which turned them into R and 8. I'll get a photo of that and show you later."

"Whatever happened to the case. Did they go to jail?" asked Sarah.

"No." said Uncle Cy, "The Minister of Justice wouldn't change his mind, because he had already said he had no jurisdiction over the thefts. The shipping companies sued Dr. Marc Arsenault and Mr. Connors in civil court. The lawyer who acted for the shipping companies was Alex Campbell. He afterwards became Premier of Prince Edward Island and later Chief Justice of the Supreme Court." *

Sarah sipped her Coke slowly, her eyes staring into space, watching the movie of the mind. Uncle Cy knew he had her seal of approval.

* This case can be found in the RCMP or Department of Justice Archives in Halifax under File No. 62H-1182-68.

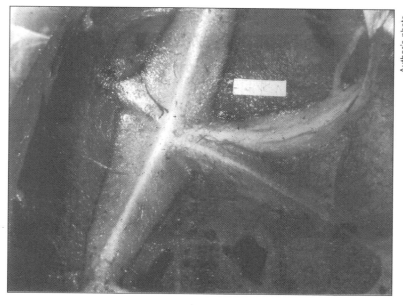

Author's photo

Initials cut in seal fat.

The Water Bomber

Everything has a way of creating space or filling it. Fire is no exception. I remember when I was a child, growing up around Deer Lake. My father, and those of my friends ran logging camps, or worked in them. In those days a lot of people smoked, and they were just as careless as people are today. Tobacco was almost a way of life. You would think that those who depended on the forest for their livelihood would have been super-careful. Perhaps smoking gave a bit of comfort to their sparse lives.

Many forest fires were blamed on lightning; even when there were no storms. But in any event they were frightening things. If you were caught on a narrow logging road with the fire roaring all around you and pieces of burning birch rhind blowing around in the wind, the need for space and comfort could not be greater. Smoke blinded everything, and the smell was suffocating. Over the years I have watched fires jump across rivers and small lakes, and even burn forward against the wind.

In the days before water bombers and organized fire services, every volunteer who could be found came to the aid of the pulp and paper companies. Mind you, they got paid a small wage but they were volunteers nevertheless.

Some years ago a friend of mine, George Pinksen, and his son volunteered to work on a fire near Deer Lake. Along with many others, they worked several days. Finally one morning they were so exhausted they lay down behind a big stump, in a relatively safe place, and fell asleep. Not long after one of the Bowater foremen came along. "Get up!" he shouted. "You're fired."

George and his son awoke, startled, as the foreman repeated himself. George drew his soot blackened self up to his full height and said, "You can't fire me, I'm a volunteer."

The water bomber really came into its own after World War II. There was a surplus of old flying boats, like the Canso, which were used on submarine patrol. Everybody was looking for a way to use these surplus aircraft. Someone got the idea that if a large tank was installed in the belly of the plane, with a 'spoiler' in front to pick up the water and a dumping device, they could be used for fighting fires in inaccessible places.

At any rate, the system was perfected and very skillful pilots used to dive down to the surface of the lakes and rivers and scoop up a tankful of water. Without stopping they would roar up from the surface, fly back to the 'hot spot', and 'bomb' it with tons of water. It was, and is, a very risky business and it takes a special kind of pilot to respond to fires in the most peculiar places. Imagine the strain on the aircraft, to say nothing of the pilot's nerves, when he or she flies that water into the belly of the plane.

Bill Smith was a water bomber pilot; perhaps he still is. He operated for years out of Goose Air Base in Labrador during the fire season. In the winter he went back to his native Scotland, where he owned a cattle farm. I hope the 'hoof and mouth' disease didn't put him out of business.

Bill always liked a joke; good pilots find it the most suitable way to relieve tension. One summer when Bill was flying out of Goose the servicing of the bombers was done by Labrador Airways. It was a bushline then, well run and innovative. They had a very good mechanic there who, despite his skill at airplanes, was a bit gullible.

One day Bill came back from patrol, taxied up to the Lab Air hangar and signaled for his favorite mechanic. When he came out to the plane, Bill pulled the release on the water tank. Out flopped two cod fish and a bunch of seaweed. "Good Lord," said the mechanic, "You must have come down over pretty shallow water!" Bill never did tell him the difference.

A few summers ago we were canoeing up the Hunt River just south of Hopedale. We stopped at Al Dand's camp at Hunt Lake and met Bill, who had just landed there. Over coffee we reminisced about old times on the Goose. Bill said he had never made such a shallow scoop for water before or since. That story shrunk the time and space between us old friends.

The Message

As many people now know, Newfoundland and Labrador became a province of Canada on April 1, 1949. We just changed our colonial masters from distant Britain, to nearer Canada. There was much uncertainty, but we all hoped it would be for the best. On July 31, 1950, the Newfoundland Ranger Force was disbanded and most of us joined the Royal Canadian Mounted Police.

Some of us became good friends with our 'mainland' counterparts. That was how I met Ray Zinck, a now famous outdoorsman, and we have been friends ever since the 50s.

Let me digress a bit; and move off, into what some would call the realm of fantasy and speculation. When we walk into a library, or our favourite Chapters, there are so many volumes on almost every subject that we scarcely know where to begin. The same applies to television, except that the programs are more selective. There's the History channel, the Discovery channel, the Biography channel and the various Religious channels. As with the authors of books, they are all pushing their particular thing; each is locked into his own particular bias. It is almost as if the authors and commentators have their own mental 'straight jackets' preventing them from escaping from the conventional wisdom of their particular 'disciplines'. My 'straight jacket' is not laced up behind, and the sleeves flap.

Just think of poor old Galileo, who became a martyr, though not in the religious sense. He used his reasoning powers and defied conventional wisdom. He was born in 1564, in what is now Italy, and died in 1642. He was what we would now call a physicist and astronomer. In Europe at the time, the Church was the fountain of all wisdom and no doctrine could be changed without its sanction. Perhaps the only thing that has changed is that the churches no longer have the coercive power to force everyone to comply. It was taught that the Sun revolved around the Earth; that is, the Earth was the center of the universe. Even a small child now knows the difference of that. Without Galileo, and if the Church had been able to retain its power, we might be sitting here today still 'professing' to believe the Sun revolves around the Earth. There would be no freedom; and thus none of the marvelous 'inventions' leading up to the exploration of space.

Galileo languished in exile and disgrace until his old buddy the Cardinal became Pope. He was given permission to write his thesis about the universe in a disguised manner. Just imagine if I had to go to the clergy to get permission to write this little book! Anyway, Galileo worked on his book for about ten years; postulating his theories through the mouths of fictional characters. You see, aside from the difficulty of composing his manuscript he didn't have a computer; or even a ball point pen. Unfortunately, one of his characters was a fool and his enemies convinced his friend the Pope that the fool was meant to be him. All hell broke loose! The bubonic plague swept through Europe, and Galileo was no longer an opponent of conventional wisdom.

Plato, an ancient Greek, who was not restricted in his thinking by the Church; because it didn't exist at that time, is believed to be the first to write about the lost city of Atlantis. Free thinkers have speculated ever since that it must have been a super civilization which spread its cultural, scientific and architectural skills to other parts of the Earth. They point to the similarities of cultural artifacts and architecture, especially pyramids, found in widely scattered places.

Ever since an army of 'scientists', all trained to adhere to the conventional wisdom of the times, have been trying to debunk this theory. They may be right; but it may be just as logical, and in time be proven, that several superior civilizations colonized remote areas of Earth. We, the various colours with our own languages, may be their offspring. Who knows what great natural, or other disaster in travel and communications, caused preceding generations to become primitive; before working their way up the chain to where we are now?

Have you ever walked into a room in a totally strange place, and felt you were there before? Have you ever dreamed about something; only to recognize that same situation later on in life? I have, but I won't bore you with the self-serving details. Rather, I'd like to tell you a story about several people that I met in later years; Zinck was one of them, and this is his story. He has agreed to let me tell it. Ray Zinck has many fabulous stories of times and events that will soon be lost to younger generations. I only wish that he would put them in a book; readers would not be able to put it down.

Constable Zinck was stationed in Hopedale in Northern Labrador for about four and a half years. While it was some years after I was in Nain in the Rangers, and used to travel to Hopedale occasionally, the conditions were similar. The coastal boat came in summer, and small boat and dog team travel were the norm. Occasionally the Royal Canadian Air Force at Goose Bay would make emergency flights in aid of local people. Communications were primitive, but there was a Marconi station at Hopedale providing contact with the outside world.

Zinck hadn't yet got to the stage of acquiring and driving his own dog team so he would hire a team and driver, usually Chesley Flowers. Ross King was the manager of the Trading Post in Hopedale and Jim Gear usually drove him around. Flowers and Gear were very able hunters; in fact they could do almost anything. I got to know them better in later years.

In February 1954, King and Zinck decided to travel to Davis Inlet; Zinck to visit his district and King the Trading Post, where Roy Hammond was the manager. They spent a pleasant few days there, visited the locals and Father Cyr, and left for home. Now ordinarily the trip from Davis to Hopedale is fairly easy, as these things go; even in bad weather you can make it in a short winter day.

It was quite stormy when they left, and grew worse as they progressed. Zinck says it was one of the worst blizzards he had ever seen. There they were, out in the middle of nowhere, with fierce winds and driving snow; barely able to see the dogs in front of them, let alone the other team. Everything was frosted up, and the dogs sheared off in the driving wind and snow. There was no trail; they knew the ice was under them because they were tripping over the crusted drifts. Chesley and Jim had a rough idea where they were, and it was decided to seek shelter.

They found an old stage, possibly built by fishermen years ago, on a small snow covered island called Malta. A 'stage', by the way, is a sort of ramshackle wharf with a small shack on it. They are not suitable for dwellings, unless you are a dead salt codfish. Now you may find it strange, but on barren land a rock or building will stand out in the snow. Because the winds scoop a saucer-like area around it, it will rarely be covered by drifting snow, except on the inside. Of course I don't mean the rock.

This Malta is not that sunny island in the Mediterranean. It was probably named by a Newfoundlander who had been to the Mediterranean with a load of fish. It is in Windy Tickle; which speaks for itself. Take a look at the map of Labrador, and you'll see what I mean. The open sea is not very far away.

You may be surprised that they didn't carry shovels; nobody did in those days. You couldn't even buy a snow shovel at the Trading Post; don't ask me why! So they dug out as much snow as possible with their two frying pans; and chopped the drifts and ice with their axes, enough to close the door. Next they tried to cover the cracks in the walls with snow blocks and whatever they could find. There was no stove; stages do not have stoves! There is no wood around Malta.

When the dogs were unharnessed, and the gear brought inside, the dogs lay down on the sheltered side and were soon comfortably snowed in. You have to see this to believe it, especially if you own a pampered house pet. Even the sealskin harnesses had to be brought in because the dogs would eat them.

Because they were only going back to Hopedale, when they left Davis Inlet, they had very little food for themselves and the dogs. They had two Primus stoves, which are fueled by kerosene, but not much to cook on them.

What can you do at a time like that? Well, you eat sparingly, because who knows how long you'll be there. Sleep? Try it in a 'see through' shack; it's only fitful, no matter what kind of a sleeping bag you have. You talk about everything you can think of; especially food; make as many stupid jokes as you can, and go out frequently to check the weather, or relieve yourself. Imagine how uncomfortable that can be!

They were stormbound for four days; it was too bad for even those hardened men to travel. The dogs didn't mind, because conditions were not much different for them. They would have liked a little more to eat, of course.

After the second day Jim Gear's easy going attitude seemed to change. Zinck asked him what was wrong, but he didn't say anything. However, he went outside more often than usual and became less talkative.

During the evening of the fourth day, Jim suddenly said, "There's something wrong back home! I got to go home right away." The others couldn't understand this, and he couldn't explain it. Zinck said, "If you go, we go. You are not going by yourself." The others agreed, and he was dissuaded from leaving right away.

Before daylight they were on their way. The weather cleared before they got to Hopedale. As they passed Black Head, and neared Hopedale, they saw a ski plane taking off. When they arrived they learned that it was an RCAF plane taking a patient to Goose Bay. Jim's second son, age twelve, was on the plane. Jim never saw him alive again; he died at Goose Bay. Jim never knew he was sick.

How did Jim know? Here was an unsophisticated person, with very little formal education. The space he occupied in this world was small; and he had never heard the theories of extra sensory perception, or anything like it. For all he knew, or cared, the Sun might have revolved round the Earth. But he somehow received a clear message that something was wrong back home. His reception and conviction was so strong that he never doubted it for a moment.

Jim Gear was right! Something, or somebody, had communicated with him. What is the explanation? I am sure that if they try hard enough, someone will come up with a 'conventional' answer.

The Counterfeiters

How easily we accept language; others, as well as our own. Perhaps a constantly enquiring mind would exhaust itself with detail and triviality. Some of us can't help it however, as we seemed to be programmed enquirers. But our enquiries are triggered; not constant, but selective. It's strange, because sometimes our immediate forbearers rarely questioned anything. But somewhere back in the distant genetic string there was someone almost like us. Almost; because in the combining and modifying genetic programs, and the accretion and variation of knowledge, the enquiring mechanism expanded. That is both the mystery and increasing benefit of 'natural' selection; people of the same sex cannot start the genetic engine, let alone drive the vehicle.

'Pro-creation' i.e. professional creation guarantees the continuation of the races; 'human', animal, vegetable; and perhaps even mineral. Without children, grandchildren, etc., our genetic chain is broken and our line will not survive. What an enormous gap in knowledge and performance that will cause!

Let us consult that imperfect fountain of knowledge: the dictionary. "Counterfeit" is defined as:- to imitate, copy, forge, pretend, sham, mislead, to resemble something closely, etc. The 'counter' is understandable; the 'feit' is not.

'Clone' is now a well known, but not fully understood word. According to Webster it means: a copy, where a descendant is derived 'asexually' from a single individual. It is wheeled out on a 'Dolly', so to speak. Is it a counterfeit? Who knows?

There has been much controversy about cloning; especially after Dolly, the sheep. Many people, some allegedly of great intellect, spoke vehemently and even sheepishly about it. Most applied conventional or religious knowledge to the problem. Others were less concerned, because it wasn't a human clone. Governments, which are of course made up of political animals, almost universally announced their intention to ban cloning. That's really surprising; because they would all want us to be like them.

Now the controversy has resurfaced; Clonaid has announced the arrival of at least several cloned humans, one of them from a lesbian. How else could such a person produce a child? Just like other childless couples, their line will die. Certain scientific commentators, who on principal see no ethical wrong, prefer to cover their beliefs and pander to the religious right by expressing fears about the health of the cloned child. It's almost as if they believed that science couldn't fix the problems in time.

Some 'intellectuals' are now crying fraud because Clonaid is sponsored by a religions cult which believes aliens from other planets are responsible for life on Earth. They forget the fact that all religions have their basis of belief in extra-terrestrial gods; intellectually there is no difference! Most people forget about the concept of 'gods' and become engrossed in the politics of the administration of religions.

The real problem in cloning anything, whether human or otherwise, lies not in the ability to produce a mirror image of oneself; but in the fact that natural genetic combinations produce ever evolving progressive personalities. When the sterile heterosexual, or the sterile gay person, allows all other things to be set aside in the overwhelming desire to reproduce an exact copy of his of her flawed self, that is a type of delusion; a psychotic narcism. All they really produce is a 'flawed' fraud; a counterfeit!

Tyrants now have the potential to create armies of human robots, in the same manner as Sony has created the robot Dog. That dog even has the ability to re-charge itself, and recognize a limited number of people. If you think in millennial terms, given this technology and its potential, we can envision the end of the human race as we know it. It doesn't make economic sense really as human beings are very cheap to produce, and relatively inexpensive to raise. But then, there is nothing rational about ego, is there?

It came in right on cue; the story of the counterfeiters, the cloners of money. Counterfeiters are egotistical too; because if they doubted their skill at evading the law they wouldn't become counterfeiters, would they?

In late September, 1959 I got a telephone call from the Manager of the Royal Bank of Canada, Main Branch, on the corner of Hollis and George Streets, near the Legislative Building, and right across the street from RCMP Headquarters in Halifax. I used to bank there; if you could call it that on my then small salary. Also, I knew the Manager very well from dealing with him on various investigations. At that time I was in charge of the Criminal Investigation Branch of the RCMP for the Province. He said it was very important.

A few minutes later I was in his office, talking to him and one of the tellers who showed me a twenty dollar banknote. She felt it was a counterfeit. Now it is not unusual for spurious money to circulate from time to time. The note looked good; almost perfect on the front. The back of the note was perfect. I turned it over and over many times until I noticed what appeared to be a smudge on the Latin motto in Canada's Coat of Arms on the front, between the two signatures. Those older notes had a scrolled motto "Amari Vsqve Ad Mare" meaning "From Sea To Sea." I felt a nervous twitch in my stomach; another mystery to solve. Would my luck hold out?

The teller said a young woman, rather shabbily dressed, had brought in the note to get some change. The teller suspected the money was bogus, because she spotted the smudged motto, and smilingly asked the woman's name. She gave it without thinking; and then left the bank immediately. I got a description, signed for the banknote, and went back across the street.

Quent Wenaus and Gene Beatty were in the office, so I assigned them to track down the woman. After filling in my boss, Superintendent Watson, I went to the Identification Branch to get enlarged photos made so that we could canvass the banks and businesses in the area. Next I made a visit to my counterpart, Superintendent Mitchell of the Halifax City Police. Together, we put our people on alert with photos of the banknote.

Successful investigations result from a combination of hard work, good memory and contacts; and the largest element, pure luck. Sherlock Holmes was not the typical detective! I always had good rapport with other police forces, the criminal element, and key people in the community. They are not always the leading citizens.

One of my neighbours, Joe King, worked at CJCH, the private television station in Halifax. He arranged for me to do a program about the counterfeit money, so as to inform the public, and shake up the culprits. Initially we thought that it was discount counterfeits, being distributed from Montreal or Toronto.

You see, the makers don't usually pass the money; it's too risky. They discount it to a gang leader, who in turn discounts it to the pushers. Sometimes it is discounted to several key individuals who travel to large cities, pass the money through small purchases; and get out. Not often are the counterfeiters caught; only the pushers.

Several days passed, and more money showed up in the Halifax area and in Montreal; the management was on my back. If you look at the photograph of Wenaus, Beatty and me, you will notice how thin I was. Actually I was very sick and on medication; a lot of the trouble was worry and lack of sleep, because we always had several major investigations on the go.

Wenaus found the girl! She was not in the phone book, but through his contacts he discovered she was a prostitute working in Halifax. He brought her in. On the surface she was very tough; but nobody is really tough underneath. I assured her she would not be charged if she cooperated, so she told us about a man she had been out with several times. She didn't know his name, or cared what it was for that matter.

Counterfeir money and plates, Halifax, Nova Scotia, October 9, 1959.

We got a good description of him and his car. She said he had been drinking heavily and when he paid her there was a big wad of money in the glove compartment. She said she didn't know where he lived. I questioned her closely to see if he had said anything which might indicate where he was from. She thought and thought and finally said she had the feeling he had some connection with Fairview; that was a suburb of Halifax at that time. We had something, but not much.

I went home, let myself in the apartment, and made a cup of tea. Shirley and the boys were asleep. They were all so used to my being gone that the boys rarely asked where I was; it was normal for me to be away. While I had cultivated the technique of shutting down my mind when necessary, I was still in thinking mode but couldn't seem to extend what little we knew. You see, investigating major crimes is sometimes quite traumatic. There are many things you want to forget when the cases are over, or even when they are ongoing; or you would never sleep. It amazes me now when I hear news reports about counselors being brought in for the most remote reasons. I guess it didn't happen in my time because no one had coined the term 'post traumatic stress'. I shut down my mind and went to bed.

Over the next couple of days Fairview kept floating to the surface of my thoughts. Meanwhile more twenties were being passed, especially in Montreal. All of a sudden I remembered! About a month before we were investigating a rape in the Fairview area. A young girl had been dragged away and raped in the vicinity of the Bayers Road Shopping Center. The culprit had worn a baseball type cap. I bought two or three dozen similar caps and had the whole area canvassed.

I did one street myself and remembered that when I knocked on a certain door, the guy came out and he was shaking and very nervous. He fitted the description given by the prostitute. I remembered the house.

Now it is very easy to convince yourself that you are right; so I thought and talked about it for a couple of days. On October 8, I didn't go home for supper, but got Wenaus to drive me to Fairview. It was raining cats and dogs that night. I told Wenaus to wait in the car and I knocked on the door. Before it opened I was almost soaking wet. A woman came out and I asked for her husband. He came out with a cup of tea in his hand. When he saw me, the cup started to rattle in the saucer; I knew he was the man.

He told his wife I wanted to see him about his work and we went down to a shabby room in the basement. I told him the prostitute had identified him; and he knew from the publicity that she had taken the counterfeit money to the Royal Bank.

Unlike you often see in the movies, I always gave a suspect the standard caution right away; read him his rights, you know. It goes like this, "You need not say anything unless you wish to do so. You have nothing to gain from any promise or favour, or to fear from any threat, that may have been held out, or made to you; but anything you say will be taken down in writing and may be used as evidence at your trial." You see, when the legal requirements are met right away, there is usually little doubt about the admissibility of a confession. Also, most suspects are more confused in the beginning than after blunt questioning.

He told me the whole story, and said that after the television program he had hidden the plates and several bundles of money. Without extracting the fine details, I asked him if he would show me where the money was hidden. There is no better evidence than that!

After telling his wife he had to go back to work, we went out to the car. I told Wenaus to say nothing, and got the culprit to direct us to where the money and plates were hidden. We went to Point Pleasant Park in Halifax and with the aid of our flashlights he uncovered the evidence near the old bunkers; we had them. Frederick John Rout went to the County Jail to dry out; what luck!

Early the next morning we arrested Colin Faulkner, and obtained a warrant for the arrest of their pusher in Montreal. He was scooped up at his hotel by our counterparts there.*

It was a strange story; all three worked at the EMI Cossor Plant in Woodside, near Dartmouth. This was an electronics plant which did top secret work for the Canadian Navy, amongst other things. Faulkner was an engineer, and Rout a graphic artist and technician. The third person was a security guard at the plant. They had a perfect cover, and used it to their advantage. When they needed photo-sensitive plates made, they went to Halifax to a large commercial photographic firm. There the work was done, at the expense of the Company, and their security guard made sure they were undisturbed. The same methods were used at the plant, where the money was made, cut and processed.

In the initial stages they made a lot of mistakes, and had to destroy about $200,000 in bogus currency. A search of the premises gave us additional evidence. Our Identification Branch matched their fingerprints on the plates and money; there was no defense.

To my knowledge, to that time, it was the first case in Canadian criminal history where the principals, pushers, counterfeiting equipment and money were all scooped up in one investigation. We did not sleep much during that hectic period.

Falconer, Rout and their guard entered guilty pleas and were sentenced to ten, nine and five year jail terms respectively. They were taken to Dorchester Penitentiary in New Brunswick to serve their time.

Author's photo

Counterfeit money.
Left to Right: Cyril Goodyear, Cpl. Quentin Wenaus and Cst. Gene Beatty.
Halifax, Nova Scotia, October 1959.

There was a strange twist in the investigation, when we began checking the management and employees of the company. One person who was employed there had not been properly vetted by our Security and Intelligence Branch. That was in the days when the RCMP ran the security service; before CSIS, the Canadian Security & Intelligence Service was formed.

Imry Nagy had come to Canada as a refugee following the Hungarian revolution. Nobody seemed to know much about him, and kept their distance because he used to smear his shaven head with garlic. He was the vilest smelling person I have ever met; I could understand why he was left alone by all in the plant.

It was well known in intelligence circles that the Soviets used to mix their agents in with refugee claimants, and thus infiltrate western countries. Canada has always had porous borders and slack systems. I discussed this matter with our management, and the S&I in Halifax. Nothing happened, and I wondered why for some time.

A couple of years later, I loaned some men to S&I to aid in surveillance of the Soviet Ambassador and his party on a visit to Halifax. These visits nearly always coincided with the arrival of Soviet 'trawlers' in Halifax; always on the heels of NATO naval vessels. We knew that there were two KGB men in the party. That evening I went down to the Nova Scotian Hotel to check on my staff. In a dark corner of the bar I caught the head of our S&I in a conversation with one of the KGB agents. Our man was a second generation Ukranian; perhaps he had close relatives still in the Ukraine. I reported the incident to my boss, but apparently nothing happened because he served a full career span and went to pension. There is much left to be explained about that, and other incidents. Perhaps that is how Nagy found employment in EMI Cossor.

In the twenty years I spent at police work, I always tried to treat even the worst crooks with kindness and courtesy. They hardly knew how to react to that type of treatment, and as a result few gave me any trouble. Rout also appreciated the fact that I tried to minimize the effect on his family. Because of this, I visited him regularly at the Penitentiary and he kept me informed as to what schemes were being hatched. He told me about three bank robberies before they even took place. One was at Plaster Rock, New Brunswick, and the others at Shubenacadie and Dartmouth, Nova Scotia.

You have to wonder at the twisted reasoning which leads people like Falconer and Rout to shrink their living space to a jail cell!

* This case can be found in the RCMP or Department of Justice archives in Halifax under File No. 59H-760-1.

The Two Dollar Murder

We have to wonder what combination of genes and circumstances creates a murderer! Where did these basic traits come from in the first place? Did the creator(s) deliberately provide the potential, or was there some scientific mistake way back when? If we revert to conventional wisdom, which embodies the belief that we were all born as innocent children, then it must be the social environment which produces the propensity for evil. Yet we know of many people, some we grew up with, who are basically timid; not an iota of aggression in them.

So, if we all came for the same source; created as we say, why is there such a variety of desires, motives and irrational behavior? Were we, perhaps, descended from those who may have been inmates of various penal colonies. Did extraterrestrial races use our little Earth in order to get rid of their undesirables? The fact that we do not yet have the means, or necessity, to establish penitentiaries in space, does not necessarily mean that it didn't happen before. Consider the origin of the term 'penitentiary', a place for confinement of those presumed 'penitent' or being coerced to appear as such.

Crimes are really the definition and classification of human acts. We do not investigate, try and convict other animals on Earth. We merely execute them without trial; even the totally innocent are the victims of hunters. Perhaps the inherent desire to kill is released in most humans through the food chain.

The most serious crimes are classified in the Ten Commandments. These were allegedly given to Moses by God on Mount Sinai, and are found in similar form in every civilization and culture. We have to presume that these criminal laws were passed down in the hope that the variety of racial descendants would have some semblance of order. Who really knows but that the destruction of Sodom and Gomorrah in that blinding flash which killed Lot's wife, severed our Earthly ties with other planets. We have to take all explanations with a grain of salt!

Here is the edited version of the Commandments; note the order of priority:

1. I am the Lord thy God; thou shalt have no other gods before me.
2. Thou shalt not make any graven image—nor bow down to them nor serve them.
3. Thou shalt not take the name of the Lord thy God in vain.
4. Remember the Sabbath day, to keep it holy. Six days shalt thou labour; but the seventh is the Sabbath and thou shalt not do any work.
5. Honour thy father and thy mother.
6. Thou shalt not kill.
7. Thou shalt not commit adultery.
8. Thou shalt not steal.
9. Thou shalt not bear false witness against thy neighbour.

10. Thou shalt not covet thy neighbour's house, nor his wife, nor his servants, nor his animals.

Any rational analysis of the Commandments should conclude that there are only two prohibited criminal acts; murder and theft. These are truly crimes in any society; the others are more likely religious and societal guidelines and are not all that profound really.

How do we get from the innocent infant to the psychopath? Is psychopathy a mental disorder; or is it a natural state based on genetics? Philosophers, scientists and medical specialists have thought, studied and debated this basic problem for centuries. Freud turned 'abnormal' behavior into a 'science'. With respect to murderers, I am 'a freud' he was wrong; as are his contemporaries.

You see, most of those experts have never dealt with murder and murderers. They gather the 'facts' and postulate their theories after the fact; mostly on a basis of sterile research. Those of us who know murderers, and have dealt with trauma in multiple circumstances, have a different view. We are professionals also, for how else could we work through those cases and continue to function as rational husbands, fathers, friends and colleagues?

We have seen the blood; the burned, decomposed and sometimes mutilated bodies. Also, and herein lies most of the trauma, we have had to deal with the relatives of the victims in their anguish. On arriving at a murder scene we shut down our emotions, and forced ourselves to view the body as another inanimate object amongst other objects. How else could we function, and solve the crime? How else could we go home, eat meat, and act as normal husbands and fathers; or deal with our neighbors and friends?

There are many things we wish to forget; and try to keep on the hazy fringes of our minds for years. But we never forget, try as we might, and they invade our normal thoughts at the most inappropriate times. Years later, like now, after rationalizing the many uneasy realities, some of us can theorize about these matters; and write about our thoughts and memories, still having reservations about the spoken word.

Murderers, or at least the vast majority of them, grow up in families and normal society. They go to school, church, and various functions and institutions and, at least in theory, absorb the same moral learning as the rest of us. Ethnic origin, nationality, language and societal location makes only minor modifications. So why do most people live crime free lives, and a minority become violent criminals? What is the real difference between a psychopath and a 'normal' person?

If we analyze the two real crimes in the Commandments, as transferred to the criminal law; i.e. theft and murder, we will find a distinct difference. Theft has many variations which are now special categories of crime; e.g. fraud, false pretenses and evasion of income tax. You see, withholding what legally belongs to another, or concocting schemes to fool people to part with their money and property, is really theft. But it is a type of theft distinct from actually taking something directly from a person; and can therefor be rationalized. The better educated the person, the higher the ability to rationalize; i.e. justify one's actions.

Many people would never think of stealing anything directly; but they do not hesitate to cheat on their income tax. The clergy, or at least most of them, would not take anything directly from the poor; but they accept donations for their organizations from the poor, and don't think about how the givers are being deprived of basic necessities. There is a mental reversal of roles where the organizations are concerned.

So the only real crime, murder as opposed to killing in self defense, seemingly cannot be rationalized. It is a strict prohibition, contrary to all codes, and taught to all 'innocents' from the cradle to the grave. Yet it seems that a small percentage of humans don't learn that basic lesson; they are psychopaths, persons without conscience and therefore unable to feel guilt. Simplistic you say, but conscience is an acquired thing; assuming that there is an ability to acquire it. Maybe the genetic makeup of a small minority precludes that ability.

As we extend the problem of killing human beings, beyond the one on one scenario, to gang executions and war, the complexities become almost endless; or do they? Psychopathic behavior can explain gang executions, because not all criminals can kill; and warriors are rationally conditioned to perform, ostensibly for a higher cause. A real case may help explain the problem.

Meteghan is a small town near Yarmouth in the heart of the Acadian south shore of Nova Scotia; peaceful, neighbourly and crime free. The odd deer is taken out of season, and fishermen sometimes cheat on their catches of lobster and scallop; not that different from anywhere else, except that Acadian French is spoken.

In the early fall of 1960, I was instructed to go to Meteghan to look into the circumstances surrounding a missing person. Two local men had come down from Ontario in order to go deer hunting. One was missing and the other was seen around town driving the missing man's car. I called Corporal Jack Baptiste to get the facts and instructed him to arrest the man on a charge of theft in order to hold him until we could look into it. I told him to hold the car and not allow anyone to touch it. Joseph Antoine Comeau was arrested in Yarmouth and held in the County Jail in Digby.*

It was a long way to Meteghan in those days but driving alone is a good way to collect thoughts and devise strategy. I arrived at Meteghan late in the evening and had tea with Baptiste and his wife; they were a nice couple. Jack had taken a statement from Comeau in which he said that he and Joseph Robichaud and been drinking all the way down from Toronto. They visited relatives in the Meteghan area and went up to Robichaud's hunting cabin. They got a deer and after a couple of days of further drinking, Robichaud disappeared. He had no idea where he was and finally took the car and drove around trying to find him. He ran out of gas in Yarmouth. Robichaud's rifle was in the car. Baptiste felt that the story could be plausible, because the two were known drunks.

The next morning we went to see Comeau in Digby. I told Jack that I would listen only, and he was to ask Comeau to tell the story for my benefit. The prisoner was friendly, joked a lot, and didn't seem to have a care in the world except he badly needed a drink. His story was substantially what he had already given in his statement. I hardly knew what to think, so we went to Yarmouth to examine the car.

Fingerprints didn't mean much, as they had both been in the car from the time they left Toronto. There was a fair amount of junk; beer bottles, scraps of food and empty cigarette packages. There were also some small traces of blood on the spare tire in the trunk. Was it animal blood?

I called Corporal Haynes of the Identification Branch, who was working in Kentville, and the following morning we went up to Robichaud's cabin about four miles from Meteghan. A relative showed us where it was. My instructions were to touch nothing; merely look. There we saw what appeared to be a shotgun blast on one outside wall and another on the outside of the door. Inside there was further evidence of shooting, but Comeau had told us that they shot up the cabin when they were drinking; that was not unusual! The cabin was a very rough thing, with a sleeping loft; it was a mess.

There were bloodstains on the ladder to the loft; badly smeared and looked as though something had been dragged up or down. There was no evidence of a deer having been cleaned in or near the cabin. We left Haynes to photograph everything, but touch nothing. Baptiste and I then went back to the County Jail.

We followed the same procedure as before, and got substantially the same story. He was still joking and very collected. We didn't tell Comeau we had been to the cabin. Then we went back to Meteghan for the night.

The next morning we were back in Digby and went through the same procedure. Comeau was now becoming anxious; he couldn't understand the silent policeman in plain clothes. After about an hour, I said, "Joe, we have been to the cabin and seen the blood and our lab people say it's human blood." I let that sink in for a while, and said, "You should, perhaps, tell us how you shot Robichaud." He hesitated, and I repeated what I had said. Suddenly he said, "Ok, I will tell you how I shot Joe." I gave him the standard caution right away. Baptiste took a pad out of his briefcase, but I nodded to him not to write anything down.

Comeau told us the same story about coming down from Toronto in the car and drinking all the way. After they got up to the cabin, and following several trips to buy beer, Comeau said he ran out of money. Robichaud wouldn't give him any, but kept talking about the money he had. Finally he gave him enough for a case of beer and when he came back they continued drinking. It was then he decided to kill Robichaud and take his money and head back for Toronto.

He took out his shotgun, fired at Robichaud and missed. Robichaud ran outside and he shot at him twice. Around the shack they went and Robichaud knelt down and begged him not to shoot. He said he shot him at close range to finish him off, but he ran inside the cabin and part way up the ladder before he died. He said he put the body in the trunk and drove him a couple of miles away and dumped the body in the woods after taking Robichaud's wallet.

As he drove away he checked the wallet and found that the only money Robichaud had was two dollars and thirty eight cents; life is cheap! The wallet was thrown out the car window. He drove around telling people that Robichaud was missing, and went to Yarmouth where he finally ran out of gas. He hoped to borrow some money, or hitchhike back to Toronto. He told us he was sorry for killing Joe; but made foolish jokes now and then.

I asked him if he would show us where the body was, and how he shot Robichaud. He agreed and I told Baptiste to say nothing, just follow his instructions. He took us back to the cabin, and reenacted the murder. The shotgun was hidden behind a mangy old sofa in the cabin.

Haynes met us at the cabin and followed us to where he dumped the body in the woods. Comeau was a small man, and he boasted how easy it was for him to carry the big body. Robichaud was wearing a woolen Mary Maxim sweater, pants and woolen socks; no boots. The sweater was unbuttoned and it was easy to see the hole in his chest. We secured the scene, did the photos and other identification work, and had the body moved to the morgue for an autopsy. I took blood samples, from Robichaud and the cabin, and the shotgun to be examined at the forensic laboratory in Sackville, NB.

We took Comeau back to Meteghan, where Mrs. Baptiste gave him a big supper. As he ate he gave us a detailed written statement about the murder. He never lost his cold blooded sense of humour. He was quite dirty, with long black fingernails. I took scrapings from his fingernails for the lab just in case.

At the autopsy it was discovered that there was a hole through Robichaud's right wrist, as well as in his chest. Because of the powder burns on either side of his chest it was obvious that he had his hands up, begging for his life. Comeau shot him at close range, through the wrist and chest. It was so close that the shot did not spread. The evidence of shooting around the cabin, and the fatal shot, ruled out the possibility of accident; no matter what Comeau might say later.

Because shotguns do not provide good ballistics evidence, and fingerprints on it could be explained, I decided to drive the exhibits to the laboratory. I caught the last boat from Digby to St. John, and drove to Sackville, where I delivered the exhibits to Madame Rouen and Peter Gazey at the Crime Laboratory.

Months later Comeau was tried by Judge and Jury at the Hotel de Ville near Meteghan. We got all the evidence in, including the scientific evidence of Madame Rouen; right down to wool fibers, resembling the Mary Maxim sweater from the scrapings under Comeau's fingernails.

At one stage it was doubtful if Madame Rouen could attend, because she was bedridden with a slipped disk. I called her and it was a very dramatic scene when she was bought up the narrow stairs into a hushed courtroom. In swinging the stretcher the attendants almost lost her, and she cried out from the pain; I don't think anything impressed the jury more than that. Comeau was found guilty and sentenced to life in prison.

You never know when these cases are over, because about six months later the Nova Scotia Court of Appeal overturned the conviction and ordered a new trial. It all hinged on what I had said to Comeau in the County Jail in Digby. You will recall that I listened to his story several times before I spoke. What I said was, "You should, perhaps, tell us how you shot Robichaud." The Court of appeal, in its infinite wisdom, interpreted that as 'instructing' him to confess; and therefore ruled that his confession was not voluntary. They ignored all the totally damming physical and circumstantial evidence, and put us and the taxpayers through the trauma and expense of another trial.

This time the trial was held in Digby before a jury and an ancient doddering Judge who could barely keep awake. That was in the days when judges were appointed for life; no matter how little life they had left in them!

This time, in my evidence, I had to say, "As a result of a conversation with the accused, he directed us to a place."

"What, if anything, did you find at this place?" the prosecutor asked.

"The dead body of a man, subsequently identified to me as Joseph Robichaud," I replied.

"Did you find anything else? asked the prosecutor.

"As a result of a conversation with the accused I located a shotgun, behind the sofa, at a cabin identified to me as belonging to Joseph Robichaud, the deceased."

"Was there anything else?" the prosecutor asked.

"Yes," I replied, "As a result of further conversation with the accused, he directed us to a spot along a dirt road near Meteghan."

"What, if anything, did you find there?"

"The accused, Mr. Comeau, got out of the police car, looked along the side of the road, and picked up and handed me a leather wallet," I replied.

"Did you determine who owned the wallet?"

"Yes, the wallet contained a driver's license and an Unemployment Insurance Card, each in the name of Joseph Robichaud. There was no money in the wallet."

And so it went; ad nauseam. Comeau sat comfortably in the prisoner's box; enjoying the show.

I spent a long time on the witness stand. During cross examination, the defense lawyer emboldened by his success in the Court of Appeal, gave me a very rough time. The jury was even squirming in discomfort. At one point, when the judge was nodding in sleep, I got fed up and said, "My Lord." He didn't hear, so I shouted, "My Lord!" He awoke, startled, and looked at me. I was mad as hell, and really didn't care anymore, so I said, "My Lord, I am not on trial here, he is," and I pointed to Comeau. "I have answered truthfully and fairly as I can given the rules that I must comply with, but I don't intend to put up with this any longer." He was so startled, he stopped the grilling.

Comeau was found guilty a second time, and sentenced to life in prison. He did not joke when sentenced was pronounced; but he never showed any remorse.

I retired from the Royal Canadian Mounted Police in 1965, with my service in the Ranger Force making up twenty years for pension purposes. I returned to Newfoundland with my family.

On September 7, 1965, I was appointed to the Provincial Court of Newfoundland. During the twenty years I spent as a policeman, giving evidence in a variety of cases in all levels of court, I learned how not to act as a judge. I continued to treat all people with restraint and respect; whether they were psychopaths or not.

Experience should always expand the space in our minds and make room for the decent treatment of our fellow beings.

* This case can also be found in the RCMP or Department of Justice Archives in Halifax, N.S. under File No. 60H-681-8.

A Full Blown Flower

We learn all kinds of things on our way through life. Much of it turns out to be useless, but interesting. Fortunately we never know whether what we learn will be useful or not, but our brains do have large storage areas where it can be filed away. The filing system is automatic, as is retrieval. Sometimes it may seem difficult, when we try very hard to remember. But if we leave it alone for a while the automatic system will function.

Since I was a child, and young adult, society has changed dramatically. Some things that we were required to do, and did in those times, are now strictly forbidden. Labour and child protection laws are fast making us into a nation of wimps. As a result we will not be able to withstand the onslaught of criminals, terrorists and invaders. My parents, as careful and loving as they were, would probably have been prosecuted by the child welfare authorities simply because of the chores we did at home; and the summer employment that we undertook with their consent.

When I was fifteen my father gave me a job with a demolition crew. He was a woods superintendent with Bowater Paper Company at the time. In those days nearly all the pulpwood for the mill in Corner Brook was cut and driven down the brooks and rivers, boomed and towed to the mill. It was part of the transportation process. Numerous brooks and rivers had dams built on them, to hold back water for the 'drive'.

As almost everybody knows, these streams are not straight and smooth. They are filled with rocks which often impeded the flow of the wood; creating numerous dangerous log jams. The crews, like the one I worked with, used to dynamite these obstacles in the summer when the water was low enough to get at them.

My boss, Mr. McIssac, was an expert with dynamite. He knew exactly what length to cut the fuses so that we would have enough time to run for shelter before the charges exploded. We would dig a hole under the rocks, place the lighted charges there, plug a few stones on top so that they wouldn't float away, and run like hell for the shelter of the woods. Between us we would rig the charges, he would cut the fuses and light them with a match. We would place two or three each at a time so that sometimes there were as many as ten charges timed to explode one after the other; the farthest first. The density of the water added to the explosive effect.

After a while, though I was always afraid, I kind of got used to it. Later we had to make up our own charges. We would open the end of the 'stick' of dynamite, punch a hole with a pointed stick and insert the explosive 'cap' which was attached to the fuse. We would then tie up the end and add however many other 'sticks' were necessary; depending on the size of the rocks. The problem was that the 'caps' were half hollow, and the fuse had to be inserted and the outer edge crimped so that the fuse wouldn't fall out. We had to crimp the end of the cap over the fuse with our teeth, and then seal it with Sunlight soap.

Every time I bit on a 'cap' I expected to be blown up. Fortunately it never happened and thus I never rocketed into space; fear makes you careful.

One of the side effects of working with such a crew was a continuous headache. The smoke from the explosions lay in the valleys and we breathed it in. I was glad when the time came for me to go back to school. While I didn't know it at the time, this knowledge and experience would be a valuable asset. I learned the difference between C.I.L and du Pont dynamite, the amount of dynamite for various jobs, the types of fuses and a host of other things. I must confess it was a great relief to me to learn later that they had battery operated detonators, which kept you a safe distance from the explosions. Today it can be done by remote wireless gadgets; another small step in the conquest of space, begun by Marconi on Signal Hill.

When I transferred from Newfoundland to Nova Scotia in the Mounted Police, I had no idea what a variety of criminal investigations would come my way. I was given the files of numerous unsolved cases which had been assigned to Corporal Stan Gardiner before he was transferred. My mainland counterparts kept telling me what a good investigator he was; I could see that. He did a lot of investigating, but solved nothing. There were several safebreaks in the files; a subject I knew nothing about!

That was when I first learned of Wesley Goldburn Harnish. It seemed that he was the prime suspect in all unsolved cases; just like the overheated stovepipe, and later an electrical malfunction, used to be the cause of all unsolved fires. He lived in a cabin on Five Island Lake, just down the old bay road outside of Halifax. That cabin was searched many times, without a warrant. I met him during one of the searches and discovered that he appeared to be mild mannered, very polite and very smart. While my counterpart was inside talking to him, I roamed around outside. Near the lake he had a kind of garbage dump, like any organized cabin owner of that time.

I found several metal containers and metal plates, which had been drilled in a peculiar pattern. One of them had obviously been blown by dynamite. From the drill holes the metal had opened outward, like the petals on a sculptured flower. Harnish was a perfectionist; he practiced his art. Because I was the new kid on the block, I didn't say anything about it. Over the next year I found that 'trademark' at a couple of safe attacks. Unfortunately, they were some distance from Five Island Lake and there was no evidential way to connect him.

Harnish was also known as 'Flannelfoot', because it was said that he used to wrap his shoes in burlap or rags to disguise his footprints. He had a lengthy criminal record and had spent many years in prison; probably why he was now so careful.

Taylor safes were all the rage in those days; probably they still are. Though with interest rates as low as they are now we would probably be better off to put our money in an asbestos sock, rather than in a bank vault. All those safes, including those designed as walk-in vaults, had a standard lock box. They varied in size, but the pattern and mechanics were all the same.

There was a dial, and inside a cast iron 'dog' to which was affixed the locking device. A good safecracker, like Harnish, had a template; and he was experienced enough to judge the variant distances in the boxes.

His tools of trade were innocuous, an electric drill, punch and pry bar; and aroused no suspicion when seen in his truck. Of course, his dynamite and 'cap' were well concealed. He would spend days scouting a place to rob; checking carefully on police night patrols. When he was ready, he would break in, drill a circular series of holes between the dial and the 'dog', punch out the piece, and place a charge in the hole. He had already calculated the exact amount of dynamite required to blow the door.

He would ignite the short fuse with a cigarette lighter, duck around a corner or into the next room. There would be a small explosion, like a vehicle backfiring, and the safe door would be open. Sometimes he would wait for traffic to go by, or a train, to cover the noise.

Early one morning, I got a call advising me that the local store in Musquodboit Harbour had been broken into and the safe blown. Gene Beatty and I drove there immediately. The back door of the store had been pried open and the office safe blown. A picture, hung above the safe, hadn't even moved. I recognized the Harnish 'flower'.

Identification personnel arrived and did their thing. We took samples of the safe 'packing' and traces of du Pont dynamite; then we headed for Five Island Lake. Harnish used to park his truck near a lonely house by the railway track. We checked there and learned he had left the day before and arrived back about 7:00 a.m. He usually stopped at the house, if they were up, but that morning he left to walk in right away.

We walked up the path to his cabin. He came outside when he saw us and invited us in; friendly and very polite, as usual. I asked him if we could look around and told him we were investigating a safebreak at Musguodboit Harbour. He politely told us to go ahead and we searched the cabin. I found a drill bit on the window sill with what appeared to be safepacking in the twist. He showed Beatty his wallet; there were several small banknotes in it and one of them seemed to have safepacking on it. I gave him the caution, but all he would say was that he had been visiting his cousins in Dartmouth the previous night. Knowing them, I felt sure they would confirm it.

Anyway, before we left, that very civilized crook invited us to have a cup of tea. We stayed and chatted with him about everything under the sun, except blowing safes. He gave me the key to his truck, asking that it be left at the house nearby.

I reasoned that since there were traces of safepacking on the floor of the store in Musquodboit, and smudged footprints; there might be traces in the truck. So I borrowed a new vacuum cleaner, bought a package of bags, and introduced a new investigative technique to Nova Scotia. I used one bag for the floor area around the clutch, brake and gas pedal, and others for the remaining parts of the truck. The mud underneath was similar to Musquodboit Harbour, but he had obviously parked it some distance away.

When I arrived at the crime lab in Sackville, I went immediately to talk to Madame Rouen. She was from

Paris, and was very, very French. By the time we got the reports back it was Christmas Eve, 1959. We went immediately to see Magistrate Martin Hayley in Dartmouth and got a warrant for the arrest of Wesley Goldburn Harnish. It was one of the meanest things I've ever done; but we had to get him off the street for the holiday season. Hayley remanded him in custody until after the New Year. With a fine sense of relief, we then went to the Legion for a quiet beer!

The case came to trial some months later and Leonard Pace conducted the defense; with Peter O'Hearne for the prosecution. Both later became judges of the Supreme and County Courts respectively. Peter was a great legal brain and an accomplished prosecutor.

The whole case was based on circumstantial and scientific evidence. Safepacking and dynamite traces found on the drill bit, money, and in the truck matched those at the scene. Harnish never took the stand to refute anything, but Pace brought in various 'experts' in an effort to discredit our evidence. He also tried to show that we had searched Harnish's cabin without authority. When I told the jury that we had stayed and had tea; that was the end of that tactic.

Dr. Shupe, a professor of science at Dalhousie University was called for the defense. The idea was to show that there couldn't be a credible match between safepacking and dynamite found at the scene and on the exhibits. The witness read from many learned volumes, as experts do, and was now reading and interpreting the report of an international study on 'diatomaceous' earth, which contains silica and is used as safepacking. For your information diatomaceous earth, in combination with an adhesive substance, is used between interior and exterior walls to fireproof safes.

The prosecution evidence was over and Madame Rouen and I were sitting back listening; I was almost bored out of my mind. Suddenly she poked me in the ribs and whispered, "I was part of that study." She told me she had been working in Australia as an independent scientist at the time and was chosen as one of the people to make the study. She scribbled a note and I passed it to Peter O'Hearne.

When the time came to cross examine, Peter led Dr. Shupe right down the garden path; puffing him up as an expert witness. He then asked the witness to read the names of those eminent scientists who had participated in the study. Shupe did just that until he got to Madame Rouen's name. Then he said, "I may have misinterpreted the data." I could have kissed Madame Rouen. She was a brilliant woman. Wesley Goldburn Harnish was found guilty as charged.

Because of his long criminal record, and the probability that he would never reform, the decision was made to proceed against him as an habitual criminal. Another lengthy hearing ensued, and he was sentenced to an indefinite period of detention in Dorchester Penitentiary.

Leonard Pace appealed his conviction and sentence all the way to the Supreme Court of Canada; and lost! I have read the decisions in the various Law Reports. It is almost as if it were a completely different matter. When these cases get into the hands and minds of remote judges, many of whom have no trial experience, it seems almost unreal to those of us who actually did the investigations.*

There was no legal aid in those days; it is a matter of conjecture where Wesley Goldburn Harnish got the money to pay his lawyer.

* This case can also be found in the RCMP or Department of Justice Archives in Halifax under the File No.59H-704-14.

Mokami

Sometime in June 2002, a friend asked what my plans were for the future. There had been a family tragedy and I was drifting in the space of my mind; in social limbo. It is not an easy thing to describe; nor did I want to. I said, "Well, in three years I'll be eighty, so whatever I do must be done before that date."

"Oh!" he said, "Is that your best before date?"

It gave me the mental jolt that I perhaps needed, and I began to think about my 'shelf life'. If you want to do anything, it is important to assess your limitations; particularly the physical. You must set your goals and hope that you can meet them. Another friend told me once that he had a five year plan. He revised it every six months, and never got anything done.

Over the years, in my work and as a tourist, I travelled across the north as far as Homer, Alaska. That is the most westerly settlement in mainland North America; Cape Spear is the most easterly. I always regretted not having seen Baffin Island, Greenland and Iceland. Now Iceland is in a different category, and I am quite sure I'll make it there prior to my 'best before' date. Maybe there is a convenient way to get to Greenland. As to Siberia? Well, I don't know!

All friends are wonderful; some even make you wonder! Mel and Sibyl Woodward extended an invitation to Ray Zinck and me to travel on their oil tanker to Iqaluit, in Frobisher Bay on Baffin Island. That tanker is one of a fleet of ships owned by the Woodward Group of Happy Valley-Goose Bay, Labrador.

Roughly translated from Naskapi to English, 'mokami' means ' a rounded hill, like a forehead'. The Inuit word for it would be 'kauk'. Mokami is a mountain half way in Lake Melville from Rigolet on the north side, opposite Northwest Islands. It has been a landmark for travellers since humans first occupied Labrador.

If you look at a map of Canada, the second largest country on earth, you will see that the new territory of Nunavut stretches from the Manitoba border and Hudson's Bay in the south, to Coppermine and along the Northwest Territories border in the west, and almost to the North Pole. In the east it shares the waters of Baffin Bay and Davis Strait with Greenland. Nunavut is a vast territory of mainland, islands and inland seas enclosing the Northwest Passage; a place of history and culture with a total population of only 27,000 people. Approximately eighty percent are Inuit. Some believe that most of the rest are from Newfoundland and Labrador. Iqaluit is the capital.

Immersed in the arrogance of our own cultures, most of us believe that other languages, particularly those labeled 'primitive', are merely descriptive of things seen and wants known; nothing could be further from the truth. All languages, if we knew them sufficiently, would be found to be full of words and phrases encompassing many conceptual things which can never be seen or fully experienced. 'Iqaluit' is such a word.

While roughly translated it means 'the fish place', it also means the river with the reversing falls where arctic char come in the thousands from the unknown ocean to spawn for the future; and to provide food for the animals and 'the people'. Many concepts flow from this word, and many stories flow from this place.

Ships plying the northern routes, especially tankers, do not necessarily operate on a fixed schedule. Ice conditions, need for fuel and topping up the tanks for the long winter, dictate when trips are made. I suspect there is a lot of calculation involved, not only with respect to volume and distance, but also weather and tides. Most places do not have docks, and floating fuel lines must be used; environmental concerns are paramount.

At 9:30 a.m. on Monday, September 16, 2002, Mel called to say that the *Mokami* was leaving at noon the following day from Long Pond, near St. John's. While that wasn't a problem for me, it was for Zinck who was living in Dartmouth, NS. He thought he couldn't make it, so Mel said he would delay the sailing in order for Zinck to get there. Anyway, between the jigs and reels he managed to get a flight to St. John's which would arrive at midnight. I had a meeting that afternoon and left Deer Lake to drive to St. John's. There was a deluge of rain the whole way, and I arrived there after midnight with my eyes sticking out like old fashioned headlamps.

When we arrived at Woodward's tank farm at Long Pond, we learned that the ship would now sail the following day. The *Mokami* and the *Sibyl* were docked there; that was my first sight of both. Compared to the *Sibyl* the *Mokami* was huge, being over 300 feet long. The *Sibyl* supplies coastal Labrador, while the *Mokami* covers the eastern arctic.

The *Sibyl* sailed first; loaded to the gunwales. She was docked astern of the *Mokami* and there was a Japanese trawler ahead, so we couldn't get out until the *Sibyl* sailed. Imagine, that Japanese trawler found it profitable to fish in our waters a world away from home; what happened to us?

We eased out through the narrow harbour mouth and began the long voyage to Iqaluit. The weather was marginal and we could barely see the headlands as we passed. At about 11:30 p.m. we passed Cape Freels and moved onward through the night. Being good guests we kept out of everyone's way that first day; there was lots of time to explore the ship.

One of the books I took to read on the trip was *The Red Limit* by Timothy Ferris. It raises more questions than answers about the universe. Being aboard the *Mokami* with sixteen other people, travelling in an inverted bowl of fog, gave me the feeling that space travellers must experience. There was nothing to be seen; no ships or icebergs, not a living thing.

Only the *Mokami* in the space of ocean and the endless hum of the engine; the creaking and other ship's sounds. Seventeen people in their own little personal world, doing their watches on the bridge or in the engine room; sleeping, reading, playing cribbage or computer games or thinking their own private thoughts. There were fourteen crew, Wade Woodward the ship's agent and fuel specialist, and two tourists. The dimension was the same; travelling alone in the space-time world in a self-sufficient ship, but really suspended until arrival time. I thought about earlier days, without means of communication, crossing the broad Pacific ocean.

The next day we explored the ship, a 3,000,000 litre oil tank; sleek and well appointed. The engine room was spotless, as was most of the rest of the ship. It is amazing what one steward and the crew could accomplish by observing a strict routine. She was built in Finland for the Soviet Union and launched on August 22, 1989 under a different name. All directions were in Russian and English. There is a sauna aboard, as well as a gymnasium; though the best exercise was walking around the deck and along the catwalk to the bow. With the weather and the ship's motion, everybody dressed warmly for their daily stroll.

One of the many things that impressed me about the *Mokami* was the fact that she is also an icebreaker, and has a seawater distillation plant. For the routes she was designed to travel it is important not to be reliant on shore water. While I can't say all the cabins had their own facilities, it seems that most of them did. Our cabins looked out over the bow of the ship and each had its own washroom with shower, desk, phone, ample closet space and a very comfortable bunk; no cruise ship could have provided better accommodations.

Mel bought the tanker in Russia and took delivery at Dutch Harbour in the Aleutian Islands. Not everyone is aware that these islands are part of Alaska and stretch about 1,200 miles from the mainland towards Asia. Older people will remember that the Japanese occupied some of these islands during the Second

World War; that prompted the building of the Alaska Highway.

The Woodward group also owns the *Sibyl* and *Apollo*, and operates the *Bond* and *Northern Ranger* under charter along the coast of Labrador as far as Nain. It is significant that they have their headquarters in Labrador. Most people don't realize that it makes more sense to be in the centre of your business area; especially when Labrador and Nunavut are your best customers. Many other prominent business families live in 'splendid isolation' in St. John's.

September 19th was Zinck's sixty-nineth birthday, so I asked Captain Ed Lawrence for permission to host a small cocktail party for those who were off duty. As it happened, Pop, the steward, and Karl were celebrating birthdays the following day; Pop would be fifty-eight and Karl twenty-five. It was a real 'ice breaker' and we were able to eat a hearty supper after. Speaking of food; there was multiple choice for each meal and plenty of coffee and snacks later, if you were young enough to eat them. The food was excellent; how easy it would be to get fat.

It is a real blessing not to be affected by sea sickness so every day was a learning experience. The crew were a well qualified and competent group; widely travelled with much experience. The chief engineer was a Russian immigrant who makes his home in Toronto. The Bo'sn was a Polish refugee who lives in St. John's, and is as close to being a Newfoundlander as possible. All the rest were Newfoundlanders including the captain, who used to sail out of southern Chile supplying the scientific bases in Antarctia.

While sailing along in the *Mokami* space ship, in that ever moving but unchanging 'fog bowl' the only living things we saw were seabirds. I used to watch them while making my rounds on deck. They constantly flew around the ship and what really surprised me was the fact that after so many wing beats they would glide. Amazingly, while gliding they would overtake the ship. It didn't seem to matter that the wind and the waves were against them, and we were moving at 14 knots. Perhaps each ocean-based colony took turns, like a relay, in flying round the ship. I couldn't really tell, because all those birds looked alike to me.

Mountains and Glaciers, Frobisher Bay, Baffin Island, Nunavut.

Author's photo

We crossed the 60th parallel at 4:00 p.m. on Saturday, September 21. That is about half way between Cape Chidley and Resolution Island in Hudson Strait. At 8:00 a.m. on Sunday we entered Frobisher Bay, and someone drew back that curtain of fog so that we could see the majestic mountains and glaciers of Baffin Island.

Baffin Island is almost 1,000 miles long, and the Arctic Circle is just marginally north of Frobisher Bay. It wasn't until 6:00 p.m. that we arrived at the bottom of the Bay and dropped anchor about a mile off Iqaluit; the 'mountain' had come to the 'fish place'. Now you may wonder why we anchored about a mile offshore? Well, there are no docks in Iqaluit and the tides rise and fall about twenty-eight to thirty feet. The Bay of Fundy boasts the highest tides in the world at twenty-two feet; well, Frobisher Bay must be out of this world.

A group of us left our 'space ship' and went ashore in a small boat. In doing so we passed a heavily loaded freighter about half way in. Captain Lawrence told us that the freighter was anchored in a deep hole; the only one in the inner Bay, and that when the tide fell it would still stay afloat.

As we walked around part of the town to stretch our legs, I noticed the usual trash you see in most northern communities along the 'landwash'. The syndrome dictates, "Never mind, boys, the snow will soon be down to cover it up." I felt quite at home.

We had 3,000,000 litres of light crude for the Nunavut Power station in Iqaluit. Light crude, with an additive, doesn't thicken in extreme arctic temperatures. Wade went ashore and advised us that there would be delay in discharging our cargo; to put it crudely. Apparently we had to wait until the power company used enough fuel to make room in their tanks; then we would top them up for the winter. Just to give you an idea how far the pipeline ran from the harbour to the tanks; the line itself holds 250,000 litres of fuel!

We went ashore again on Monday and visited S/Sgt. Ed North, who had just transferred to Iqaluit from Deer Lake. There we met a number of highly qualified Inuit people who work for the Force. In order to function there, staff has to be most versatile; all documents are produced in three official languages.

In the afternoon Rick Blennerhassett, President and CEO of Nunavut Power, gave us a tour of Iqaluit. When I asked him how many people lived there he replied, "Six thousand and twenty, and sixty-five hundred of them are Newfoundlanders."

We visited the Legislative Building, which is a work of art, and saw everything of any consequence, including the airport. That airport, as with most of the infrastructure, was built by the Americans as part of their early warning system during the 'cold war'. It is an alternate landing site for the space shuttle, with a runway of over 10,000 feet long. Rick also took us out to 'the road to nowhere' which, surprisingly, goes nowhere.

There was a tremendous amount of construction activity in town; some of it normal as it is a fast growing community, being the capital of Nunavut. But much of it was in preparation for the Queen's visit. Streets were being paved, a park constructed, and bunting flew everywhere. Thanks to the Queen, and the taxpayer, Iqaluit now has pavement.

Now the Queen is one day older than me. The story is that when my mother heard of the Queen

Mum's pregnancy, she agreed that Elizabeth should be born first. So now I was up there in Iqaluit ahead of her, sort of 'overseeing' the preparations for her visit. You would think that someone would have had the courtesy to invite me to the festivities. After all, I turned down an invitation to witness the christening of the rusty submarine HMCS *Corner Brook* in Faslane, Scotland in order to be in Iqaluit.

One of the things most noticeable about Iqaluit is that nearly all the building are on piles, or stilts as we used to call them. You can go in under most of the buildings without difficulty. It reminded me of when I was growing up in Deer Lake. There were few basements, and most of the buildings were erected on wooden stilts.

The terrain around Frobisher Bay is barren and somewhat rocky; not a tree or shrub, but there are many low arctic plants. Since the area is nearly all aggregate and rock, holes have to be drilled before the steel piles can be installed to keep the buildings off the ground. We were told that each hole costs about a $1,000; everybody goes in the hole but the contractor. The average house would need about eight to twelve holes; imagine what the Legislative Building required. By the way, the reason for this type of construction is perma-frost. Basement heat would cause some melting and the buildings would become unstable.

In the older parts of the town, where water and sewer systems are lacking, most houses have two outside insulated tanks. One contains water and the other sewage. Each tank has a red light which comes on as the tank nears empty, or full. Town staff then come around to fill up, or pump out. Newcomers walk around with raised eyebrows, until they are enlightened.

Because of my great age, I didn't go ashore every night; those off duty did. Their primary purpose, other than observing the night life, was to see what native art was for sale. There are many carvers in and around Iqaluit; perhaps the best come from Cape Dorset, and some are quite famous. Their work is outstanding! It was interesting to watch the carvers, or their sales reps, move amongst the tables in the restaurants and bars. They were always polite, never pushy, and did not lose their pleasant manner if an offer was too low; or no sale ensued. Except for the Japanese, perhaps no people are more polite than the Inuit.

It may surprise you to learn that there are no liquor stores in Iqaluit; the bars have it knocked, and I am sure they never want to see a retail outlet. The last night in town, while the *Mokami* was being pumped out, Captain Lawrence, Zinck and I went to the Legion. Now I am a legionnaire and have been in many clubs, but I have never seen a better run operation. The rules are strict, and you could see the staff knew what they were doing. Yet everything was pleasant and orderly in that great mixture of clientele; not quite the same as 'the Zoo'.

Iqaluit is a busy place and there are numerous job opportunities; they are building a capital city! There is no basic industry there as yet, only the three levels of government and their agencies. For now, it is a question of sovereignty. That has always been the fate of territories; Newfoundland and Labrador is a good example. However, these things will come to Nunavut in time; as local people learn the game, and how to assert themselves. There is a lesson in this for all of us.

One of the highlights to Iqaluit was a visit to an old friend. Many years ago in Nain I met Pauline Peyton, nee White. Her father was Richard White, a trader, and her brother is Winston White, whom many readers know. Pauline was the first registered nurse from Northern Labrador. I knew she once lived in Iqaluit because she visited Shirley and I in Goose Bay in the seventies. After that I lost track of her. It so happens that John Young of Deer Lake works at the airport in Iqaluit. He gave her one of my books.

What a pleasant afternoon I spent chatting with her, and her son James, about old times and the people we knew. Pauline told me she came to Iqaluit in 1964 to work at the hospital. Because she was part Inuit, she was not allowed to live in the nurses' residence but lived in Apex, a segregated settlement on the edge of town. You will remember that Canada was one of several countries which boycotted South Africa because of its apartheid policy; what hypocrisy!

Later she married Ross Peyton, a local businessman, and lived in one of the best houses in Iqaluit; which she still occupies. Pauline is happy in Iqaluit; it is her home. As is the tradition, she gave me two char and a piece of caribou. We had to go down to the office of Sustainable Development to get a 'Wildlife Export Permit' for the caribou. The next day we 'exported' the char and caribou at lunch aboard ship.

Meanwhile the fuel hose was put ashore and hooked up; not an easy job, and done with great skill. The wind was a strong southeast and the hose was curled around the stern line like a huge water snake.

The pumps ran all night, pushing millions of litres ashore while simultaneously filling the seawater ballast tanks.

On Thursday, September 26, the hoses were disconnected and brought aboard without spilling a drop. We sailed at 2:00 p.m. past the miles of majestic mountains with their winter caps. Gusty downdrafts blew the water along shore, like heavily drifting snow. The same three icebergs were waiting in roughly the same place to see us safely past. It blew a gale for the rest of the trip; real 'throw-up' weather. And so we sailed that 1,272 miles back to Long Pond in our simulated 'space' ship; talking, reading, working, eating and sleeping like all normal people suspended in time.

Photo by Ray Zinck

The *Mokami*.

When we arrived at Long Pond in the New Found Land on Monday, September 30, the seas were so rough we couldn't risk entering the narrow harbour. I wondered how we were going to get ashore. The boat was launched by the deck crane, but immediately began to crash into the side of the ship despite all efforts to fend it off. Now that boat is permanently fitted with a cable sling, anchored at two points fore and aft. On a signal out swung the crane and the boat was hooked on and raised to deck level. We got in with our luggage and were promptly lowered into the water. The outboard started, and we headed for the dock. Time and space are great healers.

The Road to Nowhere

He got in the Jeep and started driving across the mountains to Gros Morne. Cloud filtered sunlight shone on the peaks, and now and then a smoke-like puff of snow spiraled upward in the wind. The trees were covered from the drifting, snow and the distant forest looked as if it was sprinkled with shredded coconut. All along the sides of the road were the meandering moose tracks; made while they nibbled their early morning breakfasts. Now and then a fox or coyote track crossed them, making Chinese symbols in the snow.

The swish of the salted snow was soothing as he drove along, and he soon became his other personality; Tom. We are all schizophrenic now and then, you know! As he drove along the shoreline, a motionless gull glided along the edge of the cliff, taking advantage of the air currents. He saw the sporadic patterns in the drift ice, and the many shades from the varying thickness. The distant rocks wore glistening ice coats; as did the blasted rock faces along the highway. Amazing how those merged icicles hung there with only the grip of temperature keeping them up. Now and then the naked skeleton of an old juniper would catch his eye. They were so bare. Even the snow wouldn't stay on them; a reminder of age and death.

Author's photo

The Juniper skeleton.

Strange how the eye transferred these images to the mind; like a television program in reverse without plot, or sequence. Driving only speeded up the images, and merged some scenes while totally missing others as he was forced to concentrate on the road now and then. He remembered when he was a child, many years ago, when he used to walk on this road on the way to the logging camps. He saw no more then because the pace was slow and the road wound end-lessly; so speed really mattered only in the actual dis-tance covered, and not the sequence of images!

Now and then, as the odd car passed by, Tom would remember where he was. That was only because he was forced to push the button and wash the wind-shield. Everything else was on automatic; perhaps even his mind. He passed unknown people travelling to unknown temporary destinations for reasons valid only in their minds.

He thought about the story of the Russian, American and Newfoundlander in a bar in New York during the cold war. The first two were boasting about the scientific feats of their countries. The Russian argued that the Sputnik was the greatest achievement, while the American said it was putting men on the moon. After a while the American asked the Newfoundlander what invention impressed him most. He swallowed his beer and said, "The thermos bottle. You can keep your coffee hot, or your beer cold." The others scoffed at him. After a while he said, "You know, there's one thing about the thermos that really puzzles me." "What is that?" the Russian asked. "How does it know when to be hot or cold?" he mused. The other two had a great laugh at his stupidity.

But really, Tom thought, he was smarter than the others! They accepted everything without question; he questioned everything. His social mistake was to ask the question out loud. Those who verbalize too much, or behave in an irrational way in public, are automatically labeled by society. But what is 'rational' behavior? Who decides what is irrational?

Tom thought about Freda when he was up in Nain. She and her mother and brother lived just behind the Ranger Force building. Freda was different; rarely said anything, and stayed around her home. In the 'dead' of winter her behavior changed; whenever Tom was home at night she used to throw snowballs and icicles at the house. It got so bad he couldn't get any sleep; he even used to sneak in and go to bed without lighting a lamp. But she always knew he was there and the 'thumps in the night' would begin again. The only respite he had was to go on a long dog team patrol. He was so tormented and inexperienced he didn't try to analyze her reasons.

It got so bad that even the missionaries thought they had both gone crazy. Tom put her in a straight jacket one night and had someone look after her. However, she somehow got out of the straight jacket and nobody was ever able to figure out how.

In the summer a visiting Grenfell Mission doctor certified her as insane, and Tom took her out to the Waterford Hospital. She stayed there many years; never returning to Nain. Perhaps her life was more interesting than if she never left home.

Then there was the old man in Glovertown who said he could see movies on his clothesline. Also every time he looked in the mirror, or saw his reflection in a picture or window, he would see a monster. He'd been a hard worker and a good provider, and was still physically healthy. Why should he come to that state? Was it reality for him?

A woman in the same community so dominated her husband that he couldn't stand it any more. He called Tom and told him that when he couldn't, or wouldn't, do what she wanted she would threaten suicide. Now Tom had investigated a few suicides and knew they never told anyone what they were going to do; so he called her bluff. He remembered telling her, "Go on, go down to the back gate and jump in the harbour! Nobody will stop you." She started to cry and finally said, "No, I can't do it, I can't do it." So Tom ordered her to cook supper for her husband, and stayed there until it was ready. He never had a complaint after; police couldn't get away with that now. It solved a problem, but who knows how many more it created.

Suddenly, he saw the snowplough ahead, and came back to reality. Off in the distance the many shaped mountains marched north in their snowsuits; cold and uncaring, looking down on everyone who passed as they had from the time they were formed. Two crows argued over a Kentucky Fried Chicken box on the side of the road. They didn't move away as he passed. He drove onward with no destination.

What about the time the young fellow murdered his grandmother in Armdale, near Halifax? He stabbed her twenty-seven times with a large kitchen knife. When the Identification people were finished, Tom had to straddle the body and use both hands to haul the knife out of her and the floor; what savagery! After, the murderer got on his bicycle, drove to the McDonald Bridge, took off his clothes and folded them, and jumped over. What reasoning directed him to take two lives instead of one?

Tom's mind switched to the case in Bramber, Nova Scotia, where a gay son locked his mother in the hen-house and set fire to it. How could anyone rationalize burning his own mother? He remembered how much trouble Wenaus and Beatty had solving that case. Wenaus wore his red tie when he got the culprit to confess. He attributed the confession to the misconceptions of that time.

He remembered the young man in St. John's who seemingly had everything to live for, and was found hanging in his basement. What about the clergyman who drowned his wife in the bathtub? How could he rationalize such a breach of the Commandments? Or the pastor who panicked when he struck a parishioner's car and left the scene. She knew him and identified him for the police. That was bad enough, but in spite of the evidence he took the witness stand and perjured himself. But the day had passed when courts took the word of the clergy before all others. When cross-examination began the pastor said, "But, Your Honour, I'm a man of the cloth, surely I don't have to answer these questions." Tom remembered his other self saying, "Reverend, a man's occupation doesn't guarantee his veracity; answer the question!"

The Commandments do not forbid lying, or giving false evidence; only 'bearing false witness against thy neighbour.' It is the criminal law which forbids lying under oath. What is morality, and who is moral?

Everybody is rational in his own way Tom thought. Each one convinces himself that it's the thing to do; just like the failed businessman who believed his plan was foolproof. They are all right, at the time! The feelings of guilt, anger, pity, hope and all the various emotions kick in after-the-fact.

He stopped for lunch; for without food there is no thought. The dining room was empty, so his solitude continued. The gulls circled aimlessly over the harbour, or sat in small groups on the ice discussing something. Snowmobiles buzzed in the background, as they followed or made their own roads. After lunch he drove on; thoughts in his head bumping into each other.

Perhaps everyone, every being, moves seemingly onward; at times uncertain as to direction. It's just like looking at ants; each busily going about its business without any pattern or logic. Or it might be like looking down from a high building in a city, with vehicles of all types moving rapidly in various directions without pattern or obvious purpose.

The intelligent, the stupid, the philanthropists, the timid, the faithful, the murderers, the rapists, the bank robbers, the counterfeiters, the handicapped and the insane all move within the time-space of their lives. They walk, fly, drive or are carried, bound by gravity and the earth's orbit, even if they move counter to it just like Tom. They all have value and purpose, at least in their own minds; how else could they function? All move under the compelling force of their genetic makeup and their own thinking, however flawed, on the many roads to nowhere.

The Distant Tickle.

Author's photo